WAKING THE GIANT

THE RESURGING
STUDENT MISSION MOVEMENT

RYAN SHAW

WAKING THE GIANT

THE RESURGING
STUDENT MISSION MOVEMENT

William Carey Library
Pasadena, California
www.WCLBooks.com

Cover, Book Design and Typesetting: Hugh Pindur
Electricurrent Inc.
www.electricurrent.com

Editor: Kelley K. Woolf

Published by William Carey Library
1605 E. Elizabeth Street, Pasadena, California 91104
www. WCLBooks.com
William Carey Library is a ministry of the U.S. Center for World Mission, Pasadena, California.

Printed in the United States of America

Library of Congress Cataloging-in-Publication Data

Shaw, Ryan.
 Waking the giant : the resurging student mission movement / Ryan Shaw.
 p. cm.
 ISBN 0-87808-372-3

1. Missions. 2. College students in missionary work. 3. Missions--Biblical teaching. 4. Church work with students. 5. College students--Religious life. I.Title.
BV2063.S85 2006
266--dc22
2006034438

DEDICATION

To my mom, Karen,
who passed away during its writing,
and to my son, Noah,
who was born two and a half months after her passing.
Two generations of amazing and beloved people
who will never meet in this world!
The Lord gives and takes away...
Blessed be the name of the Lord!

I also dedicate it to my wife Kelly,
who is the epitome of a servant and of godliness.
I relish the greatness of God in my life
through giving her to me as a partner
and co heir in this adventure of faith.

WHAT LEADERS ARE SAYING ABOUT
WAKING THE GIANT

Ryan Shaw believes in the potential of youth. In *Waking the Giant* as in person, his passion for seeing all, but especially young people mobilized to the nations gives great hope that the next generation is in good hands to continue Great Commission work.

– BRUCE HUSEBY, Mission Pastor, Calvary Church

In the last few years we have seen a great need of new encouragement for rebuilding the Student Mission Movement. *Waking the Giant* is a great instrument to encourage students to be involved in mission. I highly recommend this book to Bible seminaries, churches, colleges and mission agencies to read, study, and believe that God can do another miracle and that we will see millions of people motivated and mobilized for mission today!

– NICK NEDELCHEV, President, European Evangelical Alliance

In *Waking the Giant*, Ryan Shaw sounds the mission bell for the current student generation. More importantly, he points to the God from whom we receive our global commission and challenges us to entrust our futures in *His* faithfulness. *Waking the Giant* invites the reader to understand God *rightly* – that in walking faithfully with Jesus as Lord, we must recognize His call on each of us to follow Him in complete faith, taking seriously Christ's command to preach the gospel to all peoples. The heart of God indeed beats for the nations, and this book amplifies this truth to stir awake the sleeping giant that is the student generation!

– ALEX LEE, Student Leader, Cornell University

In each generation God raises up young leaders of passion and vision with a clarion call to action that inevitably becomes a movement blessed by God. This book is the heart and call of one of these important leaders. Ryan Shaw has captured the heartbeat of God for those who are in the prime years of receptivity to the "Message Bearer" call. Read this book with an open heart and let God challenge you to Abandoned Devotion to Jesus!

— DOUG MCCONNELL, Dean, Fuller Seminary School of Intercultural Studies

---

I believe the Church is on the threshold of a major Christ-awakening movement. Having worked in the student world for decades it is no hard thing for me to anticipate that this God-given outpouring of renewal will translate, above all else, into a new *student mission movement*. This prospect is what Ryan Shaw has unpacked for us so powerfully in *Waking the Giant*. We need to hear his insights, weigh his research, heed his recommendations and embrace his hope. I've read (and written) lots of books on mobilizing the emerging generation for world evangelization. I would put *Waking the Giant* at the top of my list. I suggest you do the same.

— DAVID BRYANT, Founder, PROCLAIM HOPE!

Flowing out of Ryan Shaw's "Message Bearer" heritage and his personal encounters with God, *Waking the Giant* is a comprehensive and passionate call for students to get involved in the world's most important movement. Students who read this book will not miss our Lord's call to serve Christ to the ends of the earth and they will have practical tools to begin the journey and influence others to join them.

— GREG FRITZ, President, Caleb Project

What is it going to take to create a full-scale mobilization of students who will proclaim God's glory to the nations? *Waking the Giant* is an inspiring and practical book that challenges students and leaders to a full commitment to the Lordship of Christ and His calling.

— MIKE LOPEZ, Director, Student Mobilization, International Mission Board, Southern Baptist Convention

---

Waking the Giant is a compelling call to action to the emerging generation and to all who care about them. Drawing from Scripture, church history, his own story, and the possibilities of mobilizing 100,000 young people to pioneering missions, Ryan Shaw helps the reader envision an awesome future where today's emerging generation is challenged to live their lives and to give their lives to something much greater than themselves – declaring the glory of Jesus to the nations!

— PAUL BORTHWICK, Senior Consultant, Development Associates International

---

Beginning by looking back in history Ryan Shaw weaves a compelling vision of what Christian student mobilization in this generation could be. Personal and historical anecdotes make the book interesting to read – and the possibilities are mind-blowing!

— JIM TEBBE, Director, Urbana Student Mission Convention

In 1900 John R. Mott wrote the premier handbook of the Student Volunteer Movement, a classic volume titled *The Evangelization of the World in This Generation*. Now, a century later, Ryan Shaw has issued a fresh, clarion call to today's emerging yet potentially far more widespread Student Volunteer Movement 2. *Waking the Giant* mixes extensive research and a strong missiology with the unbridled evangelistic passion of a radical disciple of Jesus Christ. This is a book, and a cause, whose time has come.

— DAVID SHIBLEY, President, Global Advance

God put stones in David's hands; he gave Moses a rod; and to the little boy whose lunch fed a multitude he gave a few fish and a couple loaves of bread. And to Ryan Shaw he gave a book, a book that he wants to use to awaken the sleeping giant and call a multitude to action. *Waking the Giant* can be a tool used by God to awaken your spirit and stir your soul. Let God use it to give you faith for the impossible and vision to change the world.

– **FLOYD MCCLUNG, Director, All Nations**

Reflective. Comprehensive. Overdue! This book is written from the pages of Ryan's life journey and is therefore as real as it gets. But it is also wise because it reflects on the historical development of the student mission movements of former eras. This volume is as challenging and comprehensive as it is overdue. The time is certainly now for the fledgling student mission movement around the world to unite and in so doing, wake from its slumber, and move forward with exuberance and abandoned devotion!

– **DONNIE SCEARCE, Executive Director, Pioneers Canada**

This book will energize and refresh all student mission movements in the world.

SOLEMAN IRWAN, Director, PJRN – Indonesia

In *Waking the Giant*, Ryan Shaw has given us a true gift that brings clarity, challenge and hope to all of us who have a passion to see today's generation be positioned to reach all nations with the gospel and hope of Jesus Christ. This book is a must-read for anyone who cares about the gospel, the nations, and the students of today!

– **MIKE JORDAHL, National Director of Collegiate Ministries, The Navigators**

CONTENTS

FOREWORD
by Gary Witherall

In the summer of 2006, Ryan and I were with a group of students in Beirut, Lebanon. We were part of an outreach working with local believers. That week in July changed us forever as Hezbollah troops kidnapped two Israeli soldiers and war broke out. Our team was caught for several days in the midst of the unrest. All day and night we heard the roar of fighter jets and the thud of exploding bombs going off just miles away. One evening under all the noise I sat with Ryan and he told me in detail his vision. "I want to see God at work; I want to see today's generation reach the world for Christ," Ryan expressed with passion as I sat and listened.

We live in extraordinary times. It was only a few generations ago that thousands of students involved in the Student Volunteer Movement responded to the call and took the gospel to the ends of the earth. Once there, communication was slow, and supplies hard to come by. It was not a summer trip. Christian mission was shaped by young men and women who committed years of their lives. Although some died through sickness and martyrdom, they effectively touched many nations and changed Church history around the world.

Now in the twenty-first century, great advances in technology have altered the way Christian mission is done. Today we use laptops, cell phones, and the internet. Now we can fly almost anywhere around the world overnight. Information comes from every direction. Continuous news coverage has replaced the morning papers and we can find anything online, at the touch of a button. This new era brings with it additional challenges such as AIDS, economic migration, Islamic resurgence, unclean water, refugee camps and endless wars in developing nations. Then of course there are the same old issues such as overwhelming poverty, prostitution, racism and hostile oppressive regimes.

"All authority in heaven and on earth has been given to me. Therefore go and make disciples of all nations, baptizing them in the name of the Father and of the Son and of the Holy Spirit, and teaching them to obey everything I have commanded you" (Matthew 18:18-19). These were the last words of Christ to his disciples. A command to go into all the world and preach the gospel to every tribe, tongue and nation. Are you anxious to live significantly, to invest your life well? If so, take time to hear God's call through this book.

In it Ryan carefully unpacks some of the great spiritual movements revealing the power that the student generation can bring to shaping church and mission history. Like those that preceded them, SVM2 (Student Volunteer Movement 2) is summoning students to join a move of God – calling the emerging generation to stand up for the gospel. It is not about going on a summer mission trip with a local youth group, but a challenge to abandon everything and follow Jesus, and to take the gospel to the ends of the earth.

Ryan and I sat there, not far from the bombs falling over Beirut, not far from all the suffering, fury and rage. There we asked God to use us, and make our lives count.

Gary Witherall is an evangelist and much-in-demand speaker as well as the author of Total Abandon, a book which chronicles the story of living in Lebanon as missionaries with his wife, and her martyrdom at the hands of extremists.

And do this, knowing the time,

that now it is high time to awake out of sleep;

for now our salvation is nearer

than when we first believed.

The night is far spent, the day is at hand.

Therefore let us cast off the works of darkness,

and let us put on the armor of light.

ROMANS 13:11

INTRODUCTION

Dawn was just breaking as the bombs and missiles shattered the silence of a peaceful morning in paradise. December 7th, 1941; Pearl Harbor, Hawaii. Hundreds of Japanese fighter planes descended in a frenzy on America's naval fleet, most of which was docked in the harbor that morning. The planes left behind them a wake of crippled U.S. warships and thousands of dead soldiers.

History shows that this Japanese strategy was actually a serious miscalculation that backfired significantly. This unprovoked act roused the sleeping giant of the U.S. military force into World War II, completely changing the course of the war. The giant was there all along, but needed to be inspired to action.

Similarly, today's emerging generation all over the world is a giant waiting to be awakened to all that God has called it to be. I believe that history will show that the enemy's attempts to destroy, distract, and disqualify today's emerging generation have backfired. Not only will his attempts not succeed, but God in His sovereign wisdom is using the enemy's schemes to mature the emerging generation and awaken them towards their purpose and destiny of abandoned devotion to Jesus and total commitment to the global proclamation of the gospel in our lifetime.

Also, just as many of the soldiers at Pearl Harbor were young people, so I believe today's emerging generation is key in our spiritual war of advancing God's kingdom among forgotten peoples. We have had great leaders, laborers, and movements go before us and advance this cause in their generations, but our generation is responsible for what God desires to do throughout the earth in our day. The baton has been passed to us. Will we step up to take our place in the destiny of the Church?

The college campuses of the world have historically been a premier place for God to fashion for Himself laborers for the nations. The college campus is a place where young people can gather into tightly-knit communities, driven by a common purpose and pursuing a common goal. It is a place where the Lord of the Harvest has the opportunity to teach His young servants the primary lessons of faith, faithfulness, discipleship, courage, humility, evangelism, brokenness, servant-heartedness, and leadership. It is where our secret lives in God can become solid and deeply rooted. The community also provides an atmosphere where cultivating cross-cultural vision for the nations, growing in personal spiritual vitality, maturing a passion and effectiveness in evangelism, and leading and influencing others with a vision for reaching the world, are potentially experienced. When these and other disciplines are intentionally cultivated in a community setting during college, upon graduation, a multitude of prepared laborers can be released into the global harvest. These spiritually vital student mission initiatives on campuses, once networked to each other, are the widespread student mission movement necessary to accomplish the Great Commission in our lifetime.

Rice Broocks, leader of Every Nation Ministries says, "The campus has more influence on the direction, morality, and overall fabric of society than any institution on earth. Will the campuses be a starting point in a spiritual awakening that will shake the earth? The answer is a resounding yes!"[i]

In the book of Nehemiah we find a people being unified around the central purpose of rebuilding the walls of Jerusalem, and cooperating fully to see that purpose realized. The book of Nehemiah communicates four primary concepts[ii] that can help to grow and strengthen the resurging student mission movement today:

1) It highlights the rebuilding of the walls around Jerusalem

2) It introduces the reader to a new kind of leader

3) It highlights prayer as critically linked to the work of God

4) It teaches the biblical balance between dependence upon God and activity for God

The walls of Jerusalem represented the Israelites' security as a people. When Nehemiah heard that the city walls were in shambles, his heart broke. He recognized that the people were now vulnerable to attacking armies. He was a layman, employed as the cupbearer of the King of Babylon. He had no priestly duties, nor was he a Levite, but the Lord deeply burdened this man with His desire to do something about the situation of Jerusalem and her exiles. He returned to Jerusalem from Babylon, motivated his fellow countrymen for the task, and arose to see the walls rebuilt in a matter of fifty-two days! A miracle!

1. Rebuilding the Wall

I believe the time is ripe around the world to again work together toward the building of a powerful and unified student mission movement within national contexts on individual campuses and in local churches. This movement involves students, leaders, organizations, and churches all committed to the common goal of seeing the forgotten peoples reached for Jesus Christ in our lifetime.

Research concludes that the time is ripe for the effective rebuilding of a widespread and unified student mission movement in the emerging generation.* Today's movement, however, unlike the previously western-dominated student mission movements, incorporates diverse participants from many countries. Today, the global Church is leading the way and building a thriving and contagious student mission movement that cannot and will not be contained. The movement is characterized by informal national networks in countless countries made up of students gathering regularly on campuses to be challenged, prepared, envisioned, equipped and released to become global message bearers of Jesus' great love. Core characteristics of the movement include: (1) students committed to become long-term message bearers among the least-reached; (2) a deep spiritual vitality and fervor of the individuals and the groups as a whole; (3) the multiplication of campus-based prayer teams focused on the nations; (4) an emphasis on global mission vision in campuses, in local churches, and other Christ-centered communities of young people; and (5) a connection with other campus student mission groups across a given country or region creating momentum across the student world.

---

*Many statements and statistics throughout the book are based upon a research project conducted among campus ministry leaders from Campus Crusade for Christ, Inter-Varsity, Baptist Campus Ministries, Chi Alpha Campus Ministries, Every Nation Campus Ministries, and The Navigators as well as mission agencies, mobilization ministries, and Christian college campus pastors. This project researched the state and critical trends of the student mission world in North America, East Asia, and Africa.

The goal of the student mission movement includes seeing the vision of the Great Commission completed in our lifetime propelled to its rightful position at the forefront of the body of Christ's priorities. We move toward this end through the rebuilding of the student mission movement in this hour!

2. A New Kind of Leader

In Nehemiah, we find God using a type of leader He had not used previously. Nehemiah is one example of a lay leader mobilizing the people of God to a task. He was a governor who paved the way for the people to consider how God desired to use them for His Kingdom purposes. Nehemiah used his spiritual authority, not the positional authority of a priest, to influence his countrymen.

God is calling emerging leaders and leadership teams to help rebuild the united student mission movement by taking responsibility to influence their campuses and churches with the relevant challenge of fulfilling the Great Commission in our lifetime. Students do not need a recognized leadership position to influence others, but as they carry the treasure of the mystery of Christ and the burden of His calling, must learn how to share this treasure and burden with those that they live with, fellowship with and disciple. There is powerful potential for peer-on-peer influence in today's young people who are starving for leaders to look to, and will be compelled by lives that demonstrate the reality of their words.

3. The Centrality of Prayer

Prayer was critical to Nehemiah's endeavor of rebuilding. He found himself in many desperate situations where he and others had to pray in such a way that unless God intervened all would be lost. He prayed before he spoke to the king about the walls (2:4), cried out for protection from the enemies of the work of rebuilding (4:9), prayed for God to remember his labor of love (5:19), asked for strength to continue the work in light of threats from enemies (6:9), asked God to punish the enemies of the work (6:14), and confessed the sin of the people (9:5-38). The work of rebuilding the walls was sustained because of focused and fervent prayer.

Today, there are as many enemies of the resurging student mission movement as Nehemiah encountered in his attempt to rebuild the walls of Jerusalem. The hordes of hell want to keep an elevated global ministry focus from entering into the hearts of believers in the emerging generation, and so have unleashed an onslaught of self-centeredness, materialism, compromise, independence from God, immorality, self-consciousness, greed, fear of commitment, complacency, and pride, to which many have succumbed. These sins can and must be confronted in the emerging generation through ongoing prayer and intercession, if we are to see the united student mission movement effectively developed.

4. Dependence vs. Activity

Nehemiah shows us our need to depend wholeheartedly upon God as well as our need to step out and work alongside of God. God has called us to partner with Him to bring to fruition His eternal purposes in the earth. He will move in power, but He uses us broken and contrite vessels to accomplish His purposes. Therefore, we must respond with confidence that He has indeed called us, so that when trials and testing come into our lives and ministries (as they most certainly will), we will not quit.

"Unless the Lord builds the house, its builders labor in vain. Unless the Lord watches over the city, the watchmen stand guard in vain." (Psalm 127:1)

Apart from the Lord's work, we can accomplish nothing of lasting spiritual value.

Although God has called us to pray in unprecedented ways in this hour, we cannot only pray. If we believe it is God's will to rebuild the student mission movement, we will also live our lives toward that end. We will rally others on our campuses and in our local churches who believe in this movement and together work toward discovering and proclaiming God's heart-throbbing call to all-out commitment to reach the world in our lifetime.

WHY WRITE A BOOK?

There are a few reasons for which I believe the Holy Spirit has led me to write this book. The first is to sound an alarm throughout the student world regarding the reality of the collapsed walls of devoted mission commitment and vision and the desperate need of rebuilding them. We are living in critical days and cannot continue with business as usual.

Fred Markert, a noted mission strategist and base leader for YWAM (Youth With a Mission) in Colorado Springs, tells us that, "If we do not see 200,000 new missionaries raised up in the next ten years, we could be set back significantly in the cause of world evangelism."[iii] Where will the majority of these new laborers come from? From the emerging generation of devoted believers around the world willing to count the cost of following God's beating heart into the least-reached areas of the world. "*Where there is no prophetic vision (revelation), the people cast off restraint*"(Proverbs 29:1).

Secondly, I write this book to remind and encourage us of the vital role of an organized and unified student mission movement in influencing the overall missionary movement. This movement must be cultivated at a campus level, a regional level, and a national level if we are to see the missionary movement grow as it could, and together see the Kingdom of God established in places where it is not yet apparent.

I feel inadequate to answer the call to "write the vision" (Habakkuk 2:2) for today's united student mission movement, but I offer these words because I believe that the vision is vital to what God is saying to the Church in this hour. I invite us not to simply take my word for these things but commit to considering them and building on them in each of our own community contexts.

I pray that God will speak to us in a variety of ways through this book. May He activate us, to a greater degree, toward His destiny and mandate upon our individual lives and that of the united student mission world in this pivotal hour of the Church's history.

From this point on I have chosen to use different terminology to refer to certain concepts. I will replace the term "missionary" with the alternative term "message bearer", when speaking of a person involved in or seeking to become involved in global, cross-cultural ministry. This is a new and fresh term that I have found resonates with today's emerging generation. Secondly, I will use the term "forgotten" to refer to people groups or areas of the world that are currently beyond a relevant hearing of the gospel and will remain so unless a message bearer goes to them. We will discuss this concept in depth in chapter 9.

Following is a prayer made up of several Scriptures regarding God's throbbing heart for the nations. As we begin, read aloud the following declaration as a prayer, inviting the Holy Spirit to cultivate the same passion in us that beats in His heart for all people!

O Sovereign Lord, we acknowledge that because you so loved the world, you sent your one and only Son (In 3:16).

Lord of the Harvest, we know that you are the Creator of the World (Gen. 1:1). We acknowledge that your purpose is that the earth would be filled with the knowledge of the Lord, as the waters cover the sea (Isa 11:9).

Faithful Father, we know that you have blessed us so that we will be a blessing to the nations (Gen 12:1 3).

Most High God, we know that to whom much has been given, much will be required, and that the gifts you give us are to be used to serve others (Lk 12:48) (1 Pet. 4:10).

Desire of all Nations, we know that you have called us to be a light to the nations, that we would bring your salvation to the ends of the earth. We acknowledge that your name will be great in all the nations, in all the earth (Mal 1:11).

O Righteous King, we acknowledge that all throughout your word, you have shown your love for all peoples. We know that you are on a mission — a mission to extend your glory to all nations, tribes, languages and people.

- Ancient of Days, you gave us the Ten Commandments, and parted the Red Sea and saved Daniel in the lion's den, all to show your goodness and glory and to draw the nations to yourself (Deu. 4:5-6, Dan. 3:28-29, Jos. 2:9-10)

- In the Psalms, you tell us that it is your will that your ways may be known in all the earth, and your salvation in all the nations, that all the ends of the earth will fear you (PSA. 67:1,7)

- In the New Testament, we know that you have said that 'this gospel will be preached in the whole world as a testimony to all nations, and then the end will come. (MAT. 24:14)

Lord of Lords, we know that you have called your followers to go to all nations and make disciples of all peoples (MAT. 28:19-20). Lord, we confess that we have not followed this scriptural command. We confess that we've waited for you to call us again, that we've put special conditions on this command.

O Majestic One, we know that you are desiring worshippers from every culture and people. Lord, we know that in the end, people from every nation, tribe, people and language will be gathered (REV. 7:9).

Father of Lights, we acknowledge that you've called us to follow you (MAT. 4:19). We acknowledge that our attitude should be the same as yours was, that you didn't hold onto your status or comfort, but made yourself a servant. (PHI. 2:5-11)

Alpha & Omega, we acknowledge that part of the life to the full that you have promised us means following you in suffering (1 PET. 2:21). Mighty Savior, have mercy on us. By your grace, may we follow you! May your will and purpose be done in our generation (ACTS 13:36) Amen.

[i] Steve Shadrach, *The Fuel and the Flame* (Waynesboro, GA: Authentic Lifestyle, 2003) p. 185

[ii] Adapted from Robert J. Clinton, *Clinton's Nehemiah Leadership Commentary* (Pasadena, CA: Barnabas Publishers, 2002) Introduction, p. xiv

[iii] Fred Markert, *Teaching CD - Global Strategic Mission*, Crossroads DTS sessions at Kona YWAM Base, 2004

The Lord had said to Abram,

"Leave your country, your people and your father's household

and go to the land I will show you.

I will make you into a great nation and I will bless you;

I will make your name great, and you will be a blessing.

I will bless those who bless you,

and whoever curses you I will curse;

and all peoples on earth will be blessed through you."

GENESIS 12:1-3

"GOD, I PRAY THAT YOU WOULD LIGHT THESE IDLE STICKS
OF MY LIFE AND MAY I BURN UP FOR YOU.
CONSUME MY LIFE, MY GOD, FOR IT IS YOURS! I SEEK NOT
A LONG LIFE BUT A FULL ONE, LIKE YOU, LORD JESUS!"

Jim Elliot

CHAPTER 1
COULD IT HAPPEN AGAIN?

Stepping out of the Mission Aviation Fellowship (MAF) Twin Otter airplane into the middle of the dense jungle, I was greeted with a familiar smell from my boyhood: a combination of freshly cut grass, extreme humidity, and jungle vegetation. It's amazing how immediately a smell can take you back through an onslaught of memories. I proceeded down the steps of the dual propeller, 15-seat airplane, and onto the grass airstrip where throngs of local villagers waited to greet my family and me.

Thatch houses lined the grass strip on which my two older brothers and I had played as children. We had watched many Cessna 206 airplanes land and take off from this very spot. This was Hananabi, the village of 200 people in the tropical country of Papua New Guinea where I had lived for the first seven years of my life. Located in the lowlands on the Strickland Plain, near the Sepik River, about seventy-five miles from the border of Indonesia, my mom and dad had come to the Samo tribe in 1969 to translate the Bible into their language. Now my family was back to visit our friends for the first time in many years.

It was the summer of 1994. I was nineteen, and had no idea that this visit would significantly alter the direction and purpose of my life.

A GODLY HERITAGE

My family's involvement in ministry and global mission goes back three generations. My grandparents on my dad's side were both raised in godly families committed to outreach. They felt the invitation of God to go first to India with the Assemblies of God, and eventually to the Philippines as independent missionaries.

My great-grandparents and grandparents had served in India prior to World War II, and my grandparents chose to return again after the war. They, along with my dad (as a young boy), set sail for India from New York City in May of 1945, only days after the end of WWII on the first post-war civilian ship to leave a U.S. harbor, the Gripsholm. A large red cross was painted on the side of the ship, signifying to all that this was a civilian vessel, in case someone tried to violate the newly signed peace agreement.

Years later, my parents met at the University of Arizona. They married the year after graduating, in 1966. During college they had met leaders from Wycliffe Bible Translators, a mission organization dedicated to translating the Bible into unwritten languages and into dialects where there is no Scripture. They quickly recognized that this was the direction God was leading them in for their future. Their first choice of a mission field was India; Dad had loved growing up there and had fallen in love with the people. But Americans were not allowed in India at that time. The leaders of Wycliffe were looking for people to go to what was then the territory of Papua and New Guinea. Over 800 languages are spoken in this small nation, making the need for translation projects huge. So after seeking the Lord, they concluded He was leading the way to New Guinea.

My parents lived in New Guinea for twelve years. I was born in a little clinic in 1975, the year that Papua New Guinea became an independent nation. We returned to America in 1982 when my dad was asked to start a joint Fuller Seminary-Wycliffe Bible Translators program: the first Master's level degree in Bible translation.

MY JOURNEY WITH THE LORD

Though raised in a godly family, I was a rebellious boy. I tested my mom and dad at every possible point, not wanting to cooperate with them, their rules, or their standards of conduct.

At thirteen, I came to Christ and things started to change. During the summer of 1988, while sitting in a chapel at the Hume Lake Christian Center in the Northern California Sequoia National Forest, I heard a man named Dewey Bertolini give a message on the stark reality of heaven and hell. As I sat, surrounded by junior high students, I bowed my head and realized that I was not sure that I would be with Jesus in heaven if I died at that moment.

I knew the Bible, and went to church and youth group every week. Still, I didn't know God as Dewey was speaking about Him – the One who willingly surrendered all, and out of love took my place on the cross because I was sick with sin and headed for hell. I remember the agitation of my heart and soul at that moment.

Later that evening, I strolled under a beautiful array of stars, sat on an old cart in the forest, and poured out my heart to Jesus. I told Him that I had been playing games with Him and that I had not really understood His sacrifice for me. I had trusted in my attendance at church and a Christian school to save me, instead of His death on the cross, resurrection from the dead, and ascension to the right hand of God. At that moment, I recognized that nothing I could ever do to get to Jesus would be good enough, but that what He had done through the cross was completely enough for me.

Giving my life to Jesus began my transformation, but I struggled through my freshmen year in public high school with unbelieving friends who introduced me to all kinds of new and compromising situations. I found myself wanting to please God and not to sin against Him, but unable to live up to my desire.

As a sophomore in high school I became involved in my church's youth group. One night, at our weekly meeting, a volunteer youth worker, Darin Anderson came up to me and offered to hang out with me. I agreed. Over the next six years, Darin opened the Scripture to me, using God's word to show me principles of living for God, like how to hear His voice and how to be a surrendered disciple of Jesus.

When I was seventeen, I sensed the Lord calling me into ministry, but I had no idea what form that ministry would take. What I did know was that I did not want to be involved in global mission. I wanted to be involved in evangelism — serving and discipling people in North America, not around the world. During my upbringing, I had experienced things I did not understand related to global ministry that had given me a sour taste toward it. I had mistakenly equated the message bearer lifestyle with living in poverty and in my immaturity didn't understand the various forms of costs involved in serving God in global ministry or any other type. However, I had made Jesus the Lord of my life and recognized his right over me as His blood-bought child. I no longer had any say in what "I" wanted to do or be about. In fact, the "I" had to be taken out of the equation completely and replaced with "Him."

A STARTLING ENCOUNTER

One humid July morning during my visit to Papua New Guinea, I set out on a walk from our village of Hananabi to a neighboring village some three miles away. As I walked along I was not praying or thinking about God or anything spiritual. I was, however, thinking about my life and future and considering a change in majors to psychology in order to help prepare me for ministry in a local church. Suddenly, a thought flashed into my mind and a set of words penetrated my being. I did not hear the audible voice of God. But it was the closest thing to it that I'd ever heard. His words reverberated in my heart, mind and spirit, and I recognized them immediately to be from the Holy Spirit. He simply asked me, "Ryan, will you give your life for the nations of the world?"

I was startled by this encounter and struggled with it. Was this the voice of God or my imagination? And if it was the Lord, this was not the direction that I desired to take with my life. In fact, it was exactly the opposite direction I was beginning to set for myself. But I had made Jesus my Lord, and I knew that if I really loved Him and wanted to faithfully follow Him, I had to obey Him.

Over the next two weeks it became more and more clear to me that I had in fact heard the Lord speaking. I continued to fight Him, but finally, I told Him, "Lord, I want to serve You with all of my heart and I want You to use my life for Your glory. You know the issues that I have, but I want to be obedient to You and I ask that You change my heart. Jesus, I am willing that You make me willing to serve You in this way."

In doing this, I didn't ignore the very real internal misunderstandings I had held, but willingly faced them. I knew I was called to follow Jesus and embrace His plans for my life. But before I could do this, I needed Him to change my heart and give me His global heartbeat for all nations. At this point I had no desire for or attraction toward any kind of cross-cultural ministry involvement. I simply offered myself to Him, asking Him to make me willing to obediently respond to Him psychology a prayer He would answer in ways I could not have imagined.

A GENERATION ABLAZE FOR ALL NATIONS

Two years later, during the spring of 1996, I first heard the inspiring story of the Student Volunteer Movement. Sitting in Mott Auditorium on the campus of the U.S. Center for World Mission in Pasadena, California, my heart and spirit stirred as Lou Engle recounted the experiences of the Mount Hermon "One Hundred" and the student missionary movement that was sparked by these men ablaze in 1886. Lou spoke of the radical call, the movement they espoused, and of the bold watchword that became their battle cry, "The Evangelization of the World in This Generation!"

The Student Volunteer Movement had imparted to a generation of young revolutionaries a sense of commitment, life purpose, and vision that reached to the ends of the earth. Lou cried out prophetically in his trademark raspy voice, "Could it happen again? Could it happen again?" He pointed to the significance of us meeting in an auditorium named after John R. Mott, the first and most influential chairman of the Student Volunteer Movement.

As Lou spoke, a great excitement welled up within me. I visualized a revolution of young adults, ages eighteen to thirty, full of the Holy Spirit and humility, who out of a deep love for Jesus would commit their lives to reach, with urgency, the people(s) of the earth yet to hear the life-transforming message of Jesus' love, forgiveness, and power in a form to which they could culturally respond. We prayed that night and many thereafter for a mass movement among the emerging generation proportionate to today's exploding world population; that they would boldly, and in the power of the Holy Spirit, take this message globally, bringing about the fulfillment of the Great Commission in our lifetime.

GOD, WHAT ARE YOU DOING?

On a Sunday morning six months later, a man I'd only met briefly came up and handed to me a book. He explained that the Lord had led him that morning during worship to buy this book for me, and he had purchased it right then at the church's bookstore.

He didn't pray for me or anything, but just handed me a book! The book was Loren Cunningham's *Is That Really You, God?* – the story of the 1960 founding of Youth With a Mission, one of today's largest mission organizations.

I went home and began reading it that day. I reasoned that if the Lord used such an unusual set of circumstances to get this book into my hands, maybe there was a reason I needed to read it. I couldn't put it down, and couldn't stop weeping. I remember asking God why I was weeping. Something in the book was grabbing me — tugging at something deep within me. At the time I could not put words to it. Over the next six months, I reread the book at least ten times and wept each time. Through it, I began to realize God's willingness, passionate desire, and delight to use the emerging generation as vessels to accomplish His global purposes.

DEEPENING QUESTIONS

Starting in 1998, I worked with the high school and college age young adults at my local church in Pasadena, California. In this ministry, I sought to give students a vision and equip them for future involvement in global ministry. Many of them joined me on short-term mission trips to China and Peru, where they were profoundly impacted as they were used by God to bring many people to faith in Christ. This period also helped to clarify the vision of what God was asking of me.

The next year, I began studying at Fuller Seminary. While studying historical revivals and the history of the missionary movement, I learned more about the desire of God to partner with each emerging generation. I was blown away as I clearly saw how often God chose to work through a young person. Although this thrilled me initially, my excitement turned to disillusionment as I began to question what God was doing in terms of a widespread missionary movement among today's emerging generation.

Do young adults today care about, or even know about, the need for the message of Jesus Christ to get to those who have limited access to it globally? Do they understand that there are whole ethnic groups that have never heard the message? Are our fellowships, ministries and local churches encouraging the emerging generation to be involved in global ministry? What is really taking place in the "student mission world"? Are students being effectively discipled for such an end or is our form of discipleship raising up ill-prepared believers? Could we be in a time where God would waken the giant of the emerging generation into a "movement" that would powerfully impact the nations for Christ? These questions and many more began to race through my mind consistently. I knew God was asking me to do something, but I didn't know how to put these questions and convictions together into any kind of action.

One spring morning a short time later, I had breakfast with a mentor and friend Doug McConnell, Dean of the School of Intercultural Studies at Fuller Seminary. We were discussing various ministry possibilities for me after my seminary graduation, which was only a month away. I shared with him my questions about the possibility of a renewed widespread missionary movement among the emerging generation today. I knew that God was up to something, but I wasn't sure how far it extended.

Doug confirmed that God was moving in the emerging generation all over the world, gripping many with a vision of being long-term message bearers, especially those in the non-western world. He then encouraged me to contact one of his colleagues, Donnie Scearce, to look further into these possibilities.

A CHALLENGE

Donnie Scearce, director of Pioneers Canada, had been carrying a vision for more than fifteen years of a widespread student mission movement in our day that would extend beyond the Student Volunteer Movement of the late 1800s. With the various organizations in existence devoted to the emerging generation and global ministry, he felt that with common language, purpose and cohesion, the body of Christ could see an incredible exponential increase of college graduates going overseas to do long-term, cross-cultural ministry in a host of creative ways. How much more could be accomplished if we together sought to develop and communicate a common mission vision across the emerging generation, while still being faithful to the distinctives of each organization.

A month after Doug put us in touch, Donnie and I met for lunch on a sunny afternoon in Pasadena and began discussing these possibilities in greater depth. We were like two kids on Christmas morning, eager to unwrap the possibilities that lay before the student world. With faith that God had indeed arranged our meeting, Donnie challenged me to do something to put feet to this dream that we both shared. He asked if I'd be willing to travel around the U.S. and other parts of the world, meeting with campus ministry leaders, mission agency leaders, college pastors and student mobilization leaders. The purpose of the travel would be to explore the trends taking place today related to the emerging generation and global, cross-cultural ministry. The idea was to explore the issues as deeply as possible, and to get the real picture of what's happening.

My spiritual gifts primarily involve exhortation and other word related gifts. Not being gifted in administration, record keeping and details, I was hesitant to embark on this endeavor. Yet as I prayed and fasted, I was assured by the Holy Spirit that He was indeed in the midst of this, and that He would use the time spent and the information gathered from this research for His purposes. The strategies and vision of Student Volunteer Movement 2 (SVM2) – an informal network of students, leaders, churches, and organizations serving a grassroots mission movement among today's emerging generation – are the fruit of information gleaned from this project.

ENCOURAGEMENT FROM THE LORD

Two months before starting this travel, I attended a conference at which Cindy Jacobs, Director of Generals of Intercession, spoke. During one of her sessions, she spontaneously began telling stories about the Student Volunteer Movement. She then began to prophesy that God desires to rebuild this movement in our generation today, and He plans to raise up multitudes of young adults who would live among people and in places all over the world where the gospel witness was still very small. Sitting in my seat, I could hardly contain myself! It was as if Cindy were speaking directly to me. I knew that through her God was encouraging me that I was indeed on the right path and moving in the right direction.

GOD SPEAKS TO MANY

Just as exciting as God's direct encouragement to me, was the fact that He was leading not only me, but many others from many different backgrounds in this same direction. Each had their own story of how God had put the vision in their hearts, but the vision was always the same: seeing the giant awakened and the student mission movement rebuilt today around the world. It seems that when God is ready to do something new, He speaks to a number of people in a variety of circumstances about His plans and desires.

Those who will help waken the giant and rebuild the movement in today's emerging generation will be set apart from the crowd. They will not seek a name for themselves, but will do whatever it takes to challenge the emerging generation to be wakened to reach the most difficult parts of the world with the gospel. We have a choice in view of God's call. Will we continue with business as usual or will we do whatever it takes, in faith, to help steer the emerging generation into its destiny?

Scripture gives us wonderful examples of those who remained vigilant and unswerving to God, in the face of opposition. Next, we will examine two men and the spirit that they walked in, Joshua and Caleb, who stood out when ten fellow Israelite leaders backed down and didn't trust the greatness of God and His heart throbbing call in their midst.

"My name will be great among the nations,

from the rising to the setting of the sun.

In every place incense and pure offerings

will be brought to my name,

because my name will be great among the nations,

says the Lord Almighty."

MALACHI 1:11

"THE NEED OF THE HOUR IS AN ARMY DEDICATED TO JESUS CHRIST, WHO BELIEVE THAT HE IS GOD AND THAT HE CAN FULFILL EVERY PROMISE HE HAS MADE, AND THAT NOTHING IS TOO HARD FOR HIM. THE NEED OF THE HOUR IS FOR MEN AND WOMEN WHO WANT WHAT JESUS CHRIST WANTS, AND WHO BELIEVE THAT HE WANTS TO GIVE THEM THE POWER TO DO WHAT HE HAS ASKED."

Dawson Trotman

CHAPTER 2

THE TEN OR THE TWO: WHO ARE WE?

In Numbers 13, we find Israel at a pivotal point in its history. The Lord is telling Moses to send twelve spies into the land of Canaan to observe what it is like, see the obstacles, and bring back a report on the land into which the Israelites are soon to march. The children of Israel have just been delivered out of the bondage and oppression of Egypt, crossed the Red Sea, and now find themselves at what seems to be the end of their long journey in the wilderness; they are poised to enter the land God has promised them and their forefathers.

In the wilderness, God had been teaching them by His hand to trust Him for every need they had. He provided for their practical needs through the daily manna, clothes, and shoes that did not wear out. He was their only source of sustenance; He even found their water for them. He faithfully guided them with the pillar of fire by night and the cloud of smoke by day. Through all of this, He proved to His people that His guidance was perfect and that He was worthy to be trusted in all circumstances.

At the end of forty days they returned from exploring the land.
²⁶ They came back to Moses and Aaron and the whole Israelite
community at Kadesh in the Desert of Paran. There they reported
to them and to the whole assembly and showed them the fruit of
the land. ²⁷ They gave Moses this account:"We went into the land
to which you sent us, and it does flow with milk and honey. Here
is its fruit. ²⁸ But the people who live there are powerful, and
the cities are fortified and very large. We even saw descendants
of Anak there. ²⁹ The Amalekites live in the Negev; the Hittites,
Jebusites, and Amorites live in the hill country; and the Canaan-
ites live near the sea and along the Jordan."

³⁰ Then Caleb silenced the people before Moses and said, "We should
go up and take possession of the land, for we can certainly do it."

³¹ But the men who had gone up with him said, "We can't attack
those people; they are stronger than we are."³² And they spread
among the Israelites a bad report about the land they had
explored. They said, "The land we explored devours those living
in it. All the people we saw there are of great size. ³³ We saw the
Nephilim there (the descendants of Anak come from the Nephil-
im). We seemed like grasshoppers in our own eyes, and we looked
the same to the." (Numbers 13:25-33).

Ten saw only the obstacles, while two saw possibilities through the
eyes of faith. Which group do we find ourselves in? Are we like the
ten or are we like the two?

GOD HAS PROMISED US EVERY PEOPLE GROUP AROUND THE WORLD

The land was God's promise to Israel. He had set apart a people for Himself and His passionate desire was to give them their own land and inheritance, where they could worship and enjoy Him forever.

As we look at the world and the responsibility that Jesus has given us to make disciples of all peoples (Matthew 28:19), we recognize that God has promised to the global body of Christ every people group in every nation, even as He promised the land to the Israelites (Matthew 24:14; Revelation 7:9). In Psalm 2:8 the Father says to Jesus, *"Ask of Me and I will give you the nations for your inheritance, and the ends of the earth for your possession."* The nations (Greek term for ethnic people groups in the Psalm verse) are God's promise to the Son, and as followers of the Son to whom He gave His Commission, we can claim the promise of the peoples of the world finding saving faith in the love and forgiveness of Jesus Christ, as the global Church's inheritance.

It is God's purpose that all people, no matter where they live, what they believe, or what they have done during their life, have the opportunity to hear and respond to the love of His Son, Jesus Christ, in a way that is culturally relevant. This simple, yet life-transforming and all-powerful message, is our great privilege to live and share with love, compassion, perseverance, and power. Knowing this, we can equate the 'land' in Numbers 13 with every place around the world where the gospel has yet to go and where the church has yet to be planted. It is God's wholehearted desire for us, His children, to cross cultures and extend His glorious message to all people who have yet to experience its reality.

The Difference Between the Ten and the Two

What was the primary difference between the two groups of spies in Numbers 13? Each of the twelve were Israelites, beloved of God, spiritual leaders, with the promise of the land before them. What was the heart condition that separated Joshua and Caleb from the ten unfaithful men?

The God of the Impossible

The natural circumstances and realities of what the spies had seen in the land made what God had said He would do seem impossible. The people were strong, the cities were fortified, and giants inhabited the land. How could the Israelites think that they could conquer this land? In Matthew 19:26, *"Jesus looked at them and said to them, 'With men this is impossible, but with God all things are possible!'"*

It is the will of God, at certain times, to place us in situations in which the only way that we can possibly prevail is if He intervenes. In this way, He alone receives the honor for the victory, and He teaches us to trust Him the next time a seemingly impossible situation arises. Many of us, however, rarely step out in faith because we fear that we will fail, and we end up missing the joy of partnering with God and seeing Him triumph.

While on a recent trip, my wife Kelly and I found ourselves in such a situation. We were about to board a bus that would take us from Sarajevo, Bosnia to Belgrade, Serbia. We had exactly the right amount of local currency left to pay for the tickets, and then we were out of Bosnian money as we were leaving Bosnia for another country. We paid for the trip at the ticket counter and proceeded toward our bus to load our luggage. As we approached the driver to give him our luggage, he asked us for an additional 6 KM Bosnian currency for the luggage. He spoke no English and demanded the 6 KM if we wanted our luggage to go along with us. We had no Bosnian money left, our host in Bosnia had already left the bus depot, and there was no nearby place to exchange money. We were stuck with no way to pay for our luggage to be brought along. Suddenly, a man behind a gated area about one hundred yards away began shouting at us and motioning us over to him. We had no clue who he was, so we ignored him, assuming he was trying to get the attention of someone else. He persisted, however, and the people around us confirmed that he was speaking to us. I hesitantly walked over to the gate and without a word he placed in my hand exactly 6 KM. He then motioned me away from him. Who was he? Why did he give us this money? There was no way he could have overheard our conversation with the bus driver to know the exact amount needed. Kelly and I gave honor to God for His faithful and unexpected provision, paid the driver, and loaded our luggage.

Consider the mountain that stands before the followers of Jesus in Bosnia. According to the best estimate among local message bearers, there are about 800 true believers throughout this nation of four million people. In the centrally-located town of Travnik, there is only one known national believer in a population of 35,000. In the beautiful lush valley where Travnik is located, there is only one church fellowship of fifteen believers out of a population of approximately 100,000.[i] To see the gospel proclaimed, the Kingdom of God take root, and the body of Christ in that area grow, the Lord must intervene in power through message bearers willing to serve in such a location.

Among some people groups in nations like Libya, North Korea, Saudi Arabia, Syria, Vietnam and others around the world, the situation is even bleaker – and paints a picture of hopelessness and seeming impossibility. Yet, as it did for the Israelites of old, the promise of God remains. Although the prospect of seeing the church planted in these and other nations may seem daunting and, at times, impossible, Jesus has promised that He will do it and use us as His vessels. But we must obey Him and step out in faith.

He has also promised, *"All authority has been given to Me in heaven and on earth"* (Matthew 28:18). What a promise, made in the same sentence as the Great Commission! Because of His sacrificial work on the cross and resurrection from the dead, all authority and dominion, lost by Adam at the fall, was stripped from Satan and fully restored to Jesus. Jesus longs to release this authority to us as we plant churches in areas where there is no viable gospel witness.

The Increase of God in Dark Times

Though it sounds strange, I get encouraged when my mind wanders to the immensity of the global task still looming before today's advancing Church. The ways of God throughout Scripture teach us that it is when something seems utterly impossible, that we can expect God to use drastic means to bring forth His will and purpose. He is truly on a mission in the earth today! When darkness and sin abound, as we see in our world today, *"His grace increases all the more"* (Romans 5:20).

Take Joseph, in Genesis 40, as an example to us as he sat in prison in Egypt after God had spoken to him years before about his destiny and calling. Dark times indeed! Here was a young man with an incredible purpose from God before him; yet he was in jail having been accused of sexually assaulting the wife of the second highest official in all of Egypt. But God was with Joseph and used the situation to test his integrity and build his character. In His perfect timing, God brought him out of jail and thrust him into national prominence and total favor with Pharaoh for the purpose of saving many through his wise grain storage (Genesis 39:21).

Or consider Paul and Silas, sitting in jail praying and worshipping God when suddenly an earthquake erupts, completely shaking the prison, opening the door and breaking off their chains (Acts 16: 25-26). In a similar fashion, God can break through our dark situations and times in a moment.

We Can Reach the World in Our Lifetime

I firmly believe that today's global Church can reach the world for Jesus in our lifetime. We are living in extraordinary times! God is moving around the world with increasing visibility. Though the outlook in many places may seem daunting from our finite viewpoint, I see at least four reasons to believe that we could realistically see the literal fulfillment of God's global purpose in our lifetime.

First, the Church is presently making tremendous headway in this direction. From 1974 until 2004, the number of those around the world who were out of reach of the gospel message have been reduced from one-half to one-third of the global population.[ii] This means that in a thirty year time-span the Church was planted in almost as much territory as in the first 2,000 years of church history.

Second, the number of those around the world who put their faith in Jesus for salvation in the decade of the 1990s was tremendous. In several parts of the world the percentage of people coming to Christ greatly increased over the decade of the 80s.[iii] We can believe that this will only continue in the years ahead as the global Church is mobilized for the final push in world evangelism.

Third, technology is multiplying the ways that the message can be distributed. Take the tiny Islamic island country of the Maldives located off the tip of India, for example. During a visit to this beautiful country, known as the scuba diving capital of the world, I asked a twenty-year old Muslim man to, "Tell me about the various beliefs of people on the islands." He responded with firmness and ease, "Everybody here is Muslim. Nobody is anything else!" The idea that someone could have a different outlook was totally foreign to him. I later discovered that for the first time in the nation's history, gospel messages had begun to be beamed in by radio from Sri Lanka (shortly thereafter, the government realized this and scrambled the air waves). The technological possibilities before us are truly astounding. Similar stories are common of people using MP3 players to record training materials or the New Testament to be read aloud for illiterate people, as these have a large capacity for storing digital memory.

Fourth, the Church is learning strategic, focused intercession and is beginning to understand how to move in the authority of Jesus boldly, yet wisely. In the 1990s, millions in the global Church were mobilized through the 10/40 and 40/70 window prayer initiatives, praying for the gospel of the Kingdom to take root throughout the most resistant areas of the world. Luis Bush relates, "Praying through the Window III in 1997 focused on the unreached people groups… nearly 27 million intercessors from 121 nations prayed for the lost of the window."[iv] This type of intercessory prayer unleashed continually throughout the global Church, is the predecessor of breakthrough and an unprecedented harvest.

In the 1700s, a phenomenal prayer movement took place in the Moravian community of believers in Hernhhut, Germany. They established what came to be called the "one hundred year prayer meeting"— day and night prayer in which people committed to pray for various time slots day and night. At least one person (usually more) was consistently crying out to God for a one hundred year time period! Signs, wonders and great conviction of sin from the Holy Spirit were unleashed and multitudes came into the Kingdom as a result of this worldwide saturating prayer. New waves and expressions of this movement began in the United Kingdom and the United States in 1999: "24-7 Prayer" and "IHOP – International House of Prayer". They are ongoing prayer movements among the emerging generation that combine creative expressions of prayer and intercession with passionate cries to God for revival.

During a ministry trip in Lagos, Nigeria, I was invited to attend an all-night prayer meeting and evangelistic service held in a huge, open field on the outskirts of the city. The denomination that hosted this gathering did so on the last Friday night of every month. I had no idea what to expect, but went with much curiosity. When my host and I arrived by car, I was utterly astonished as I made my way through a sea of 1.2 million Nigerians who had come to this gathering. There were many prolonged times of corporate intercession focused on national revival and global evangelization throughout the 12-hour meeting. The global Church is learning to pray en masse, and as a result, walls of bondage and deceit are being shattered as we move forward in this hour.

Serving Out of Weakness, Not Strength

To see the world reached, however will take a major shift in our outlook. Most of us examine our strengths in light of how God might use our lives globally. We ask questions like, "What am I gifted in?" and "What am I passionate about?" These questions are helpful, but they can also be misleading. They are all about us when the global work to be done is all about Him. Instead of becoming activated in God out of our strengths, Jesus calls us to answer His invitation in our weakness. This is difficult for most westerners. I believe, however, that today's generation is uniquely equipped to do this, partly because of the brokenness in our midst. God uses weakness, not strength. In our strength, we strive. In our weakness, we trust and depend upon Him in humility!

In talking to a message bearer in a forgotten area, I asked what she thought it was going to take to see the Kingdom established in Arab countries. She emphatically declared, "A humility on the part of laborers and a willingness to be rejected, talked about, mistreated and scorned, and for these not to give up and think God is calling them elsewhere, but to respond with Jesus' love and forgiveness each time. If laborers can do this for years without seeing much fruit, the locals will watch this and begin to respond, and over time transformation will take place."

Two well-known American mission leaders were invited to Saudi Arabia to talk with leaders in the royal family. When they arrived, they were ushered into the chambers of the palace and sat before one of the members of the royal family. For the next two hours the Saudi royal ripped into Christians generally and America specifically. He angrily criticized the practices of what he understood to be consistent with Christianity. The two visitors sat without uttering a response. Finally when the leader asked, "Do you not have anything to say in defense?" one of the men began weeping, and with tears in his eyes said, "Will you please forgive us for the hurts and atrocities that we've caused you? By doing as you say, we were not being obedient and faithful to God!" The royal was speechless. He didn't know what to say to such a response. He was waiting for the two men to lash out in defense of Christianity and America. Instead they modeled the meekness and humility of Christ in their reply.

The Scripture teaches that it is through our weakness that we are actually made strong (2 Corinthians 12:9; Hebrews 11:34). We serve in an upside-down kingdom where the first shall be last and the last shall be first (Matthew 20:16 and others). We are called to embrace and have confidence in our weakness and the greatness of God, not in our strength.

Satan's Opposition

In Numbers 13, the obstacles that the twelve spies found in the land were very real. They were not made up or overly dramatized. The obstacles were many and, to the ordinary person, overwhelming. The sense of futility of going into the land must have filled their hearts and minds as they looked upon the vastness of the people and the strength of their fortifications. Parallel to this, we see the very real opposition today to the work of the Great Commission.

It doesn't take much to realize that Satan is currently working overtime around the world with his purpose of stealing, killing and destroying (John 10:10), and holding people in darkness and hopelessness. This should not surprise us. The last thing Satan wants to do is to allow the Kingdom of God to be established in locations around the world where he has dominated for centuries.

Yet the power of God seems to be increasing in significant ways simultaneously, to outdo and overcome the deception of the enemy in these days. Isaiah 59:19 says, *"When the enemy comes in like a flood, the spirit of the Lord will lift up a standard against him."* The Lord is positioned, as He was for the Israelites on their brink of crossing the Jordan, to go before us as we step out in faith and place our assurance in Him to make a way where there seems, in the natural realm, to be no way.

The Reality of Islam

One of the many major strongholds in Satan's camp today is fundamental Islam. There are close to 1.24 billion adherents to Islam

worldwide, comprising one-fifth of the world's population.[v] However, as is true of the estimated number of Christians globally, we
know that not all of these Muslims are fundamental, devout or even
practicing their faith. Many are Muslim in name only.

Evangelism among Muslims is complicated because Muslims believe
that to forsake Islam is to not only forsake their religion, but also
their country, family, ethnicity and culture. Talking with a young
Muslim in Bosnia, I inquired about his background and religion, and
he mentioned he was Muslim. I then asked how often he prayed five
times daily, went to the mosque, gave alms and if he kept the Rama-
dan fast. He grinned at me rather sheepishly and said, "Hardly ever
and no!" I then commented, "And you still say that you are Muslim."
His response was, "Oh yes, I am Bosnian and so I am Muslim." This
same story could be repeated over and over from nations throughout
the Muslim world.

The Muslim world has only in the past fifteen to twenty years
become even a small focus of the global Church's strategy.[vi] So few
Muslims found faith in Christ for hundreds of years that most believers thought Muslims were impossible to reach. This attitude is changing
as the Spirit of God is whispering into listening ears that He is able and
desperately desires to break into the hearts of Muslims with His love.
Certain mission organizations like Frontiers, Arab World Ministries,
and Ministry To Muslims have focused their efforts entirely on the
Muslim world and have been learning how to live among, serve, and
effectively plant churches among these beloved people.

Over the past decade a spiritual hunger has enveloped many parts
of the Muslim world as multitudes are seeing the emptiness of Islam
and its inability to bring true peace. In fact, more Muslims have come
to faith in Jesus Christ since 9/11 then in the previous 200 years of
outreach to them.[vii] Powerful stories of Muslims finding true faith

in Jesus have been circulating to encourage the hearts and intercessions of many in the Church. Many of these are stories of Muslims
receiving dreams in the night and open visions during the day of Jesus
or angels speaking to them. We need more message bearers willing to
go and live in the Muslim world at this critical time.

Since 9/11, there has been a heightened fear, based mostly in ignorance, of the Muslim world. This is simply another tactic that the enemy has used to keep the Church from striving to seek out Muslims
with the Gospel. Yes, there are very real issues that we now face, but
in reality, the number of adherents to a fundamental or fanatical form
of Islam is relatively small. Most Muslims would not align themselves
with these groups.

We have tended to make assumptions about Islam as a whole based
on what we have seen of a few Muslims (the ones that generally make
the evening news). In the same way, Muslims have tended to make
assumptions about the West in general, and America in particular,
based on what they see portrayed of the West on television, in movies
and on the internet. The vast majority in the Muslim world are kind,
friendly, extremely accommodating and not prone to violence. They
are as misinformed about westerners as westerners are of them.
(For books on Islam see the Recommended Reading List in Appendix A).

God's Test

God's test to us who would follow after Him and seek to serve Him
around the world is this: Will we allow our circumstances to dictate our
response to God's will, as the ten spies did, or, will we put our faith in
God's promises and His ability to accomplish His will, as the two did?
Those who do not wholeheartedly want to serve God or who believe
that "God is not able to overcome in my situation" will fail the test.

God is going to do what He has promised. The only question is whether we will get to be part of what He's doing by responding in faith and confidence, or be disqualified from the joy and reward of participating in His end-time harvest because of our unbelief. There are many believers who are in the latter group. Let us confess our unbelief and ask Jesus to help us overcome it (Mark 9:24).

G. Campbell Morgan writes in his commentary on Numbers, "At this moment in very deed the whole land is before us. What are we going to do? Everything depends on whether we see the walled cities and the giants or God. Nothing less than a triumphant faith, born of a clear vision of God Himself, will enable us to go forward. It is only faith which can cooperate towards infinite issues. Sight can do small things. Faith alone is equal to infinite things!"[viii]

There will be a generation which partners with God and realizes the fulfillment of His global promises. Why not ours? Why not now? Let's step out in belief trusting our faithful and unchanging God who has promised to make the way and whose will and purpose it is to advance His kingdom in triumphant victory.

THREE HINDRANCES TO "TAKING THE LAND"

In Numbers 13 the ten weren't willing to go into the land because of (1) Fear, (2) A small vision of God and (3) Lack of perseverance. Today, these same conditions can hinder the emerging generation from embracing its God-given global responsibility.

FEAR

This fear took on a host of faces for the Israelites: fear of the unknown, fear of the known, fear of lack of provision once they entered the land, and the fear of real danger.

...Of the Unknown

The Israelites' fear was born out of knowing very little about the peoples who occupied the land. The spies had brought a report, but this only gave them a physical description of the land. Though God had promised victory, He hadn't shown the Israelites how they would practically walk out that victory.

Similarly today, we are afraid as we consider going to new places with cultures different than our own. We ask ourselves, "Will I fit in? Will the people like me? Will I like their food? Will I be able to easily adapt to their customs? Will I learn the language adequately? Will loneliness overtake me? Will I be homesick? Will I have a real spiritual impact? Will it really matter that I am there?" For too many of us, we give up and never make it over the obstacle of these most elementary and common questions.

A group of message bearers recently moved to a forgotten area of northern India. For some time they have been committed to going to this particular group of people entirely devoid of the gospel, yet had struggled with some of the same issues mentioned above. Their biggest fear was that they wouldn't have a spiritual impact. They asked, "Will we get there after preparing for so long and praying so hard for these people and not be able to effectively share with them about the love of Jesus?" This was a real question for them, and yet they would not let such a fear hold them back from what they knew God was asking them to do.

...Of the Known

The second area of fear rises from what we do know about "Going" to the nations. The Israelites knew that they were smaller than the inhabitants of the land, outnumbered by them, and would have the difficult role of foreigners invading those who were comfortable and secure in their homes. These were not points in their favor for winning the battle!

Similarly, as we step out, many of those around us may think we are out of our minds. Our parents, friends, professors, bosses, or church leaders might not understand the choice we've made to serve God in this way, and they may be less supportive than we had imagined and hoped. We cannot base our decisions on what others think – doing so can sideline us, cause us to miss the will of God, and worst of all, grieve His loving heart.

Jesus tells us, "...*there is another who testifies in my favor and I know that His testimony about me is valid...I do not accept praise from men...How can you believe if you accept praise from another, yet make no effort to obtain the praise that comes from the only God*" (John 5: 32, 41, 44). It is the Lord Himself who must testify of us. This takes place as we draw nearer to Him in intimacy, friendship, and total surrender and we subsequently sense His pleasure over us, and His peace within us. The views and thoughts of the Most High, not those around us, is the only view that counts in the end.

...Lack of Provision

God is the one who is the source of all of our provision, protection, and sustenance. If we truly understand this about Him, then we will not fear that somehow He will not take care of us as we go forward to do His will. The temptation to cling to financial security is real for every believer who seeks to serve God in cross-cultural ministry. We should not ignore it, but instead proactively, "...*submit ourselves to God...and resist the devil and he will flee from you*" (James 4:7).

We ought to resist the temptation to doubt God, and respond instead with a childlike trust in His never-failing character. He has promised us that as we go forward with confidence in Him, being led by His Spirit, He will make the way for us. It is not our job to figure out how He will work everything out, but, rather, with whole-heartedness to believe that He will do so. This will not come easily, and many times our faith will be tested, but through the difficulties God will develop in us character, perseverance and dependence on Him alone. Remember that He is a jealous God and wants to be the only One in whom we trust (Deuteronomy 4:24).

A few years ago, I was preparing a group of high school and college students for a short-term ministry trip to China. One of our students was short $800 to pay for her trip. The night before the official financial deadline, she was contemplating what to tell me concerning her involvement. The next morning she checked her mailbox and found an envelope containing exactly eight one hundred dollar bills with no note attached. To this day, we have no idea who gave this money. God is able to meet our needs in unexpected ways when we place our confidence in Him alone.

...Danger

There are very real dangers today to being involved in cross-cultural ministry. The world is getting darker, and Satan's stranglehold is getting tighter, but the work of God remains unfinished. I want to suggest that our media does not portray the world accurately, but are instead making situations appear story-worthy. The seemingly dangerous places we see on TV are not nearly as risky as they may appear. Knowing this, it is our responsibility to go onward wherever He may lead, ultimately putting our safety and our lives into God's hands.

Even in the most difficult and potentially hazardous places we must get God's perspective. Though the price may seem high, history shows us that the blood of the martyrs is the seed of revival. It is predicted that this year 160,000 believers worldwide will be martyred for their faith.[ix] Some of us will be used to glorify God by dying for Him, but let us remind ourselves that most of us have been called not to die for Jesus, but to live for Him.

Friends of mine, Gary and Bonnie Witherall lived in Sidon, Lebanon, where Bonnie worked as a pre-natal nurse in a clinic with Palestinian women. On a typical morning in November, 2002, she went to work and was met by two Muslim extremists who decided that they did not like the young woman volunteering her time to help others in the name of Jesus. They shot her three times in the face.[x]

Gary was obviously crushed by the loss of his young wife. After taking time off to grieve and to process this monumental crisis, he sensed the Holy Spirit leading him to begin sharing Bonnie's story with college students across America as a testimony of someone willing to do whatever it took to see the message of Jesus' love taken to those who have the least opportunity to hear it. Bonnie was a woman who loved deeply and would not allow fear to interfere with her love of Palestinian women. Many young adults have responded to God's call to absolute surrender as a result of Bonnie's tremendous courage and willingness to place her life in God's hands and pay the ultimate price out of a heart of love.

It is Jesus who exhorts us, *"If anyone comes to me and does not hate his father and mother... yes, even his own life, he cannot be my disciple. And anyone who does not carry his cross and follow me cannot be my disciple"* (Luke 14:26,27).

We know that Jesus is not encouraging the hatred of ourselves or of those closest to us, but rather, is advocating a devotion to Himself that supersedes all other relationships and loyalties. We are not tied to those around us, even those closest to us, but are bound to Jesus alone.

John heard the voice of God declare how believers will ultimately walk in the final victory over Satan's opposition: *"They overcame him by the blood of the Lamb, and by the word of their testimony, and they did not love their lives so much as to shrink from death"* (Revelation 12:11).

We are God's people and He wants us to live in complete surrender to Him, grasping the purpose of our lives- to enjoy and love Him with full hearts and serve Him, not ourselves – even if this means placing ourselves in seemingly dangerous situations. Places that seem to us to be dangerous are not always so. Someone once said, "The safest place you can be is in the middle of God's will, wherever that may be."

Do Not Fear

God knows that fear is our natural response to the unknown, so He tells us, "DO NOT FEAR" fifty-eight times in the Bible. In Joshua 1, God commissions Joshua to lead the Israelites into the promised land. Joshua was evidently afraid of this new role and responsibility, but instead of rebuking him, God tells him four times, *"Be strong and courageous...For the Lord your God will be with you wherever you go."* (Joshua 1:9)

It is the Lord Himself who fights on our behalf when we surrender to His will. What comfort, strength and courage to a fearful heart – beyond mere feelings, we can press on with a heart-believed recognition that the God of the universe is with us. Does the powerful presence of God mark our lives and ministries?

HAVING A SMALL VISION OF GOD

According to Numbers 13, the second primary hindrance we find for the ten spies was that they had a small vision of God. They only allowed themselves to see the opposition and forgot who it was that had called them. They placed more confidence in the power of their enemies than in the power, the promise, and reality of Almighty God.

In 2 Kings 6: 13-17 Elisha the prophet and his servant are surrounded by the army of the Arameans who are positioned to attack and destroy them. The enemy numbers are frightening, but Elisha's response to the real fear of his servant is, *"Don't be afraid! Those who are with us are more than those who are with them."* The servant must have thought Elisha was out of his mind! It was clear that this was absolutely not the case, and it seemed that they would be crushed by the opposing army.

In verse 17, Elisha prays, *"O, Lord, open his eyes that he may see."* Then the Lord opened the eyes of the servant, and he looked and saw the hills full of horses and chariots of fire all around Elisha!" The army of the Lord had encamped around the enemy army, and the Lord then blinded the enemy army and gave the victory to the Israelites. The land can be taken! Those who carry a true revelation of the power and greatness of Almighty God can penetrate hostile nations with the Kingdom of God.

Over the last few years, many prayer-walking teams have gone to Morocco to pray blessings over this Islamic nation, and asking God to move in creative ways. A few months passed and the lead singer of the Christian band, the Newsboys, received a phone call from the Moroccan government inviting his band to come and play a tour of concerts in every major city in Morocco. The Islamic government recognized the bad influence that western pop culture was having on Moroccan young people. In response, they wanted to bring in a western band that would appeal to their young people, yet had wholesome lyrics and values that matched their own, so they chose a clearly Christian band.

God is so immense that we could live a thousand lifetimes and still not come to grips with His trustworthiness and faithfulness. We need to move away from the small vision that many of us hold of Him, and embrace the magnitude of the reality of who He is, what His character is like, and what He is about. The primary way to grow in this is by deliberately studying God's word and meditating on His greatness in the Scriptures. May we ask the Holy Spirit to release the revelation of the vastness, character, and love of the Most High into our hearts and show Himself to us in a fresh way through the Bible!

It is not enough to simply give mental assent to God's greatness. As Paul teaches, true belief takes place in the heart, *"...if you confess with your mouth, 'Jesus is Lord,' and believe in your heart that God raised Him from the dead, you will be saved"* (Romans 10:9). It is heart belief that God is after.

A LACK OF WILLINGNESS TO FIGHT AND PERSEVERE

The ten spies brought back a report that not only included, but emphasized, the obstacles before them. Recognizing the task would take serious work to accomplish, they decided it wasn't worth it.

Planting the gospel in a place that has been entrenched in the enemy's kingdom is not going to be easy or quick work. Most of us like things easy. We look for ways to cut corners and to find shortcuts. Because of our laziness, the mere difficulty of a certain task causes many of us to avoid it. The global proclamation of the gospel among the forgotten cannot be completed quickly or easily. We must get our hands dirty to do this work.

It will not happen overnight and we need to ask God for steadfast, decisive, and firm hearts to, "... *throw off everything that hinders and the sin that so easily entangles and let us run with perseverance the race marked out for us"* (Hebrews 12:1). God is calling a generation that patiently commits to the task for the long haul, doing whatever it takes to see the Church planted globally.

DISOBEDIENCE VS. OBEDIENCE

We know that in the end, the negative response of the ten spies influenced the Israelites to grumble and complain against Moses and God, choosing to be disobedient concerning God's purpose of going into the promised land. God saw this and was grieved that they did not believe, trust, and obey Him. He responded by declaring forcefully that none of that generation of Israelites, except Joshua and Caleb, would ever enter the land.

The people were forced to spend forty more years going around the mountain until that generation had died off. Then a new generation was given the opportunity to respond with faith and obedience to God's command. They did respond with humility and faithfulness and we know that as a result, Joshua led the people into the promised land, and they were victorious in taking it (Book of Joshua).

Will we, as a generation, respond to the call and command of God to go into all the world with the gospel and make disciples? Will we emulate the traits that Joshua and Caleb demonstrated as they believed and trusted in God and His commands? Or will we respond as the ten did, with fear, a small vision of God, and blatant disobedience? Will we be passed over, as Moses' generation was, grieving God and missing His will? Let us rise in obedience, choosing weakness over strength, faith over unbelief, confidence over fear, a large vision of God over a small one, and perseverance and discipline in the face of difficult situations.

As I write, stories of those who are responding like Joshua and Caleb are being written all over the world. Individuals, churches, campus ministries and other communities are rising up to meet God's cry for all out faithfulness and obedience in this hour. Next, we will look intently at biblical and historical models of God's passionate desire and commitment to use the emerging generation for His purposes. These are the historical peers of today's emerging generation and have much to teach us today.

[i] Personal Interview with Pioneers Team in Bosnia — June, 2004

[ii] Mission Frontiers website - http://www.missionfrontiers.org/newslinks/statewe.htm

[iii] Joel News website - http://www.joelnews.org/news-en/jn440.htm.

[iv] Luis Bush & Beverly Pegues, *The Move Of The Holy Spirit In The 10/40 Window* (Seattle, WA: YWAM Publishing, 1999) p. 31.

[v] US Center For World Mission website - http://www.uscwm.org/mobilization_division/pastors_web_folder/global_mission_statistics.html

[vi] Greg Livingstone, *Planting Churches in Muslim Cities* (Grand Rapids, MI: Baker Book House,1993) p.39

[vii] Mark Gabriel, *Islam and the Jews* (Lake Mary, FL: Charisma House, 2003) p. 187

[viii] G. Campbell Morgan, Handbook For Bible Teachers and Preachers (Grand Rapids, MI: Baker Book House,1994) p.18

[ix] Houston Perspectives website - http://www.houstonperspectives.org/missiontrivia.html

[x] Gary Witherall, *Total Abandon* (Wheaton, IL: Tyndale House, 2005) p.5.

Let no one despise your youth,

but be an example to the believers

in word, in conduct, in love, in spirit, in faith, in purity.

1 TIMOTHY 4:12

"THIS GENERATION IS WAITING FOR A CHALLENGE THAT WILL DE-
MAND THEIR ALL. THEY ARE WAITING TO FIND SOMETHING TO POUR
THEIR LIVES INTO- SOMETHING TO SINK THEIR TEETH INTO. THEY
HAVE BECOME DISILLUSIONED WITH BOTH THE SECULAR WORLD
AND THE CHRISTIAN WORLD. IT IS TIME TO CALL THEM TO GIVE
THEIR LIVES AWAY FOR A CAUSE GREATER THEN THEMSELVES."

Ron Luce

CHAPTER 3
GOD LOVES THE EMERGING GENERATION

The historical development of the missionary movement is filled
with stories of men and women who, responding to the leading of
the Holy Spirit, went throughout the earth as the hands and feet of
Jesus Christ, declaring in word and deed the Kingdom of God. Many
of these caught the vision of God's work globally while still in their
teens and early twenties, and began their ministries straight out of
college or university. The emerging generation throughout history
has made a tremendous impact on the missionary movement.

Biblical Examples

From the earliest pages of Scripture, God has used the emerging
generation in reviving His people and bringing forth His purposes.
Often we overlook the fact that many of the heroes of faith in the
Bible were young men and women. We picture them as decrepit, yet
even Jesus' disciples were probably no older than their mid-twenties.

David was a young man when he was anointed king by Samuel
(1 Samuel 16), though he didn't assume the role for many years. Yet his
courage and faith before Goliath as a seventeen-year old changed Israel's

history forever. This courage was motivated by his unwavering desire for the glory of God to be known in all the earth (1 Samuel 17:46).

Daniel was a young teenager when he was taken from his homeland and thrust into the alien society where he would live the remainder of his days (Daniel 1). Forsaking the temptation toward bitterness, he made a conscious choice to trust the Living God as he faced incredible challenges to his integrity and faith. Because he passed the test with flying colors, God raised him up and gave him tremendous favor and godly influence in a pagan kingdom

Let's not forget the primary role of a young woman named Mary in the redemptive drama. She was probably only fourteen years old when asked to forsake her reputation and embrace the scorn and misunderstanding of friends and family for the purpose of being the one to bring the King of kings into the world. Who would believe a young woman who said she had conceived and was with child by the Holy Spirit? I've often wondered why the Holy Spirit chose such a young woman as Mary for this vital role. He could have chosen an older woman to bear Jesus. Yet He seemed to be teaching us that He is committed to those who will respond to His call in faith, no matter their age! He loves to use the foolish, simple, and humble things of the world to confound the wise (1 Corinthians 1:27).

Another example is Jeremiah, who was about twenty years old when God called him to be His prophet. The Lord's caution to him in Jeremiah 1:7 could also be a prophetic challenge to today's young adults: "Do not say, 'I am a youth,' for you shall go to all whom I send you, and whatever I command you, you shall speak. Do not be afraid of their faces for I am with you to deliver you!" God knew Jeremiah's response long before he could even think such thoughts. He knew it would be a fearful thing for a young man to step out and be His mouthpiece to Israel…yet He called him anyway!

Many scholars believe that Stephen, a man full of faith and of the Holy Spirit, who did great signs and wonders among the people (Acts 6) was a young man in his early twenties when God used him to condemn the Pharisees and temple priests through his powerful speech showing how God had led the people of Israel since the days of Abraham. Israel had consistently and stubbornly disobeyed God   stiffening their necks as He sought to form them into His image, but out of His great love for them, God had sent Jesus as a ransom for their heaped up sins. The Jewish leaders were enraged at Stephen's rebuke; they accused him of outright blasphemy and stoned him to death.

Timothy is another scriptural example of one who, in his youth, fixed his eyes upon loving and serving His Lord, no matter the cost. He was mentored by Paul and traveled with him, watching and learning from all that Paul did. He was then given the opportunity of setting out on his own to lead the church in various communities. God commissioned him to be His mouthpiece among His people.

David, Daniel, Mary, Jeremiah, Stephen and Timothy were ordinary, even imperfect people, just like us! One of the primary messages of the Bible is that God delights to take blemished people and make them into His mighty warriors. This is a great encouragement to those of us who think we are too ordinary to be used for God's great exploits!

Historical Examples

History paints an equally clear picture of God's love to anoint the emerging generation to accomplish His purpose:

> JOHN CALVIN found Christ at the age of twenty five and a year later wrote *The Institutes of the Christian Religion*, which became a theological classic.

GEORGE WHITEFIELD began to preach at the age of twenty-one and soon surpassed his elder contemporary, John Wesley, in profile.

DWIGHT L. MOODY planted a youth church in an old tavern in the heart of Chicago while still a young man.

CATHERINE BOOTH and her husband William founded the Salvation Army. She had read the entire Bible eight times by the age of twelve.

EVAN ROBERTS was twenty-six years old when God called him to lead the Welsh revival from 1904-1906. This awakening began in a youth meeting with young adults pleading with God for breakthrough and an open heaven. He answered!

CHARLES SPURGEON became the most popular preacher in London by the age of twenty-one.

BILLY GRAHAM'S worldwide ministry started through post-WWII youth rallies to which young adults came by the thousands to hear the young man preach.[i]

Hudson Taylor, founder of China Inland Mission (known today as OMF or Overseas Missionary Fellowship), first sailed for China in 1853 as a twenty-one year old. He faced many struggles as a young man in this setting, but he persisted, believing that God alone, not a person, had called him.

Taylor saw that most of the work being done in China was limited to the coastal areas, to the utter neglect of the inland regions teeming with Chinese who had no chance to hear the gospel message. Sensing strongly that God was placing upon him this responsibility, he returned to England to appeal to others to come and join him in focusing on the inland regions of China. Many recent college graduates did, and the China Inland Mission was founded – all because a young man put himself in a position to be used of God in spite of severe setbacks, one of which was people on every side telling him he was crazy. The China Inland Mission was the first mission organization to be called a "faith mission" based on the fact that Taylor trusted God for all of the financial provision for the mission and its workers.[ii]

Bruce Olson is another example of a young man allowing God to use him for His purposes. As a teenager in the 1960s, Bruce caught a vision for his involvement in cross-cultural ministry, and his heart began to beat for the Indian tribes of South America who, at that time, were out of reach of the gospel. He contacted many mission agencies and organizations through which he hoped to be sent, but each of them turned him down, stating that he was too young and had no experience.

Undeterred, Olson decided that God Himself had called him and that he would not allow men and their structures to hold him back. Thus, at the age of nineteen, Bruce Olson set out alone for the nation of Columbia, not backed by any church or agency, trusting in God alone for provision and guidance. Olson faced real hardships, but persevered, and today there is a vibrant, mission-sending church among the Motilone Indians, to whom he went.[iii]

Why the Emerging Generation?

While God will use anyone of any age who is available to Him, there is clearly a special place in His heart for the young adult who is abandoned and devoted to Him.

> [13] I write to you, fathers, because you have known Him who is from the beginning. I write to you young men because you have overcome the wicked one. I write to you little children because you have known the Father.

¹⁴ I have written to you, fathers, because you have known Him
who is from the beginning, I have written to you young men
because you are strong and the word of God abides in you, and
you have overcome the wicked one..... (1 John 2: 13-14)

John is highlighting the strength, energy, and vigor of young adults, given to them by God that they may bring Him glory through accomplishing His purposes. These verses also confirm that God has ordained the defeat of the enemy to come from the spiritual authority that has its source in devotion to the word of God. Those who are hungry for the Holy Spirit to change them, form them in character and Christ-likeness, mature them, strengthen them, discipline them, and teach them, are ready to be used of God and enter the spiritual fight that is before them.

The Current Generation's Opportunity

I am excited beyond imagination for this current generation of young adults. Why? Because they have been privileged by God Himself to be alive today, facing the challenges and struggles of our corrupt and dangerous world. They are His voice, hands, and feet in what might be our final effort in seeing disciples made and the world reached. It is not an accident that it is they who are alive in this hour, and not Hudson Taylor, Amy Carmichael, Jim Elliot or a host of other past message bearer heroes. God has handpicked this generation for this hour – the nameless and faceless who make up half of the world's population.

There is, however, no victory without a fight. As we are well aware, the enemy has been working overtime to destroy the emerging generation.

Hell sometimes seems to know better than the Church the
critical nature of the hour. Yet in every case heaven's own
promised deliverer has escaped the sword and the flame

and lived to visit the vengeance of God on the enemies of life and love and destiny. In our time the war has come again. One-third of your generation never even made it out of the womb. Sixteen million in America alone fell victim to abortion, never given a chance to make any kind of a mark on a world they never saw. Of those who lived, half have had to survive the disintegration of their families, the bitter breaking of marital bonds meant to shelter and sustain them. You are survivors of a siege against divine destiny. As before hidden somewhere among you is a promised child that has escaped the dragon. Only this time, there's not just one, but many. And they will take the battle to the end of the world."[iv]*-Winkey Pratney*

Satan is the author of strategic destruction. He seeks to destroy that which threatens him. The current generation seems to be up against one of the greatest onslaughts Satan has ever waged. Yet the Spirit of God is not deterred. The brokenness in our midst could be the very thing that qualifies this generation for power ministry. Recognizing the reality of a shattered life and the offering of it to a Holy God requires great humility. When we draw near to God in humility, we position ourselves to receive a measure of His grace, which cannot be obtained any other way (Proverbs 3:34).

I am in no way condoning the reckless release of wounded people. What I am proposing is that God in His remarkable mercy and grace is using for good the very thing the enemy meant for evil (Romans 8:28)! Throughout Scripture, is not the heart of God drawn especially near to those who are hurting and broken-hearted? And are not those who are forgiven much also those who love much (Luke 7:47)? True brokenness is a right understanding of our fallen state in light of the grace of Almighty God.

Revival and Expansion of God's Kingdom

Paul Pierson, professor of Church history at Fuller Seminary, says that in the history of the Church, true revival in one location and subsequent geographical expansion of the Kingdom of God around the world have always gone hand in hand.[v] Global geographical expansion of the Kingdom is the natural result of the revival and renewal of His people.

In 1904 a revival broke out in Wales. The little nation was brought to its knees by an awareness of the literal presence of God everywhere – in shops, factories, mines, taverns, music halls, trains, and schools. Revival meetings were marked by an intense awe that settled over those gathered. Many times the leader, Evan Roberts, could not even get up to preach because the weight of the glory of God filled the meeting room. The power and holiness of God hovered over the nation. It wasn't only believers who experienced the reality of God, rather, hundreds and thousands found faith in Jesus during the two years of uninterrupted power.[vi]

Stories of what was happening in Wales reached almost every nation and raised the faith level of believers everywhere. Many went out as message bearers to reach a dying world as a result of their hearts being awakened to God's love for the world, and they reaped a harvest of disciples to Christ.

Through this awakening, a small (it doesn't take many to move the heart of God) group of both black and white believers, the integration of whom was rare in those days, began to pray fervently in Los Angeles that a similar outpouring would fall upon them. They didn't have to wait long. In 1906, the Azusa Street revival broke out, and from this historic outpouring, the global Pentecostal movement was born, sending masses of message bearers into the nations empowered for service.

Recognizing the critical relationship between revival and the missionary movement, we must seek God for a present outpouring of Biblical revival. It is through spiritual awakening that the Church again recognizes Jesus' rightful place as her head, and allows Him to live through her to accomplish His global purpose. *(For a listing of recommended books about revival, see Appendix A)*

The Emerging Generation's Role In Mission

As we saw with Hudson Taylor and Bruce Olson, the history of the missionary movement bears abundant witness to God's passion to use the emerging generation. Most of us need to be continually reminded of the ways that God has used young adults as His vessels. I am convinced that many in this generation don't now how He has used others of their same age to do extraordinary exploits in His name. We need to grasp God's desire to use young people if we are to move forward effectively. When we allow this fact to spill over into our hearts, our faith is boosted to envision God accomplishing His will through our lives and our generation. We don't have to wait until we become "of age" to be used of Him. God is preparing in us hearts that He can trust to hold the concerns of His own heart.

STUDENT MISSION MOVEMENTS – THE LAST 200 YEARS

How many of us are aware that college students have been at the forefront of every major historic mission thrust? Most of the traditional faith mission agencies of today, including Overseas Missionary Fellowship (OMF), CIM, WEC International, RBMU International, SIM International and Africa Inland Mission were founded by radical young people with a vision of global harvest. It was through students that the missionary movement from North America was initially birthed two hundred years ago.[vii]

In America, the first seeds of student involvement in the missionary movement were sown on a little college campus tucked away in the woods of western Massachusetts in 1806. The end of the eighteenth century found many colleges slipping from their biblical foundations. This low spiritual climate was the backdrop for the Second Great Awakening. The Awakening was brought on through a group of believers who had had enough of the low spirituality and called for fervent prayer against society's ills. God answered with a mighty downpour.[viii] This Awakening moved across the Church as a whole, but had a profound effect specifically upon the colleges of the day. In 1802, Yale put out a report that stated that *one-third* of their students had found faith in Christ.[ix] Radical prayer became a normal part of the students' lifestyle. Entire days were regularly set apart totally for prayer.

THE HAYSTACK PRAYER MEETING

In this setting of spiritual fervor, five students met regularly in 1806 to pray in a grove on the Williams College campus. On one summer day, a thunderstorm forced them from the grove to find shelter under a large haystack where their hearts were arrested in prayer for an awakening of global mission interest among their fellow students. Samuel Mills, the leader of the five, had been reading William Carey's book, popularly called *Enquiry*. Carey is commonly known as the father of the modern missionary movement who sailed to India from England in 1793. His writing stirred the Church in England, and Samuel Mills as to their responsibility in global mission. Mills' heart was deeply pierced by the things this message bearer was saying.[x] He shared the Biblical concepts he had been pondering with the others. While praying, each determined in their own hearts to become message bearers. Their watchword became, "We can do this, if we will!"[xi]

These prayer meetings continued as the five students influenced other students to consider serving God overseas.

In 1808 they organized formally, launching the Society of Brethren, a group of members bound together by the vow to give themselves to extend the gospel around the world and to keep each other to this purpose through thick and thin. The Haystack Five confronted many of their classmates with God's beating heart for the nations, pressing each one to make commitments to become involved in cross-cultural ministry once they graduated.

This was the first ever student mission movement on a college campus in America and the forerunner of what God desires to do on multitudes of international campuses today. From 1810 to 1870, 527 students on multiple campuses joined the Society. Of these, about half made it overseas as message bearers.[xii] According to David Howard, "In 1856, there were 156 colleges and forty-six theological seminaries in the United States. Seventy of these colleges had Christian societies of one sort or another. Of these, forty-nine had societies which designated foreign missionary emphasis."[xiii]

It is important to note that in 1806, no mission organization, agency or denominational mission board was in existence in America! America's involvement in the missionary movement had not yet begun. The Haystack students approached various denominations asking them to set up a board, which would send them out as message bearers. Many turned them down, but finally the first North American mission board was founded – the American Board of Commissioners for Foreign Mission.[xiv] It was through the prayers, intercessions and influence of five students that the American missionary movement began.

Principles for Today

There are several key principles we can glean and apply to our own campuses from what took place at Williams College through the Haystack prayer meeting.

1. Perseverance Pays Off

These five recognized the centrality of prayer and its relation to laborers being raised up for the Kingdom (Matthew 9:37-38), and were willing to boldly advocate this idea that was new and not well-accepted at the time. What might happen in our spheres of influence if we commit ourselves with perseverance to prayer for the nations and for laborers to be raised up as we spread the vision of God's global purpose in our communities?

2. Peer-on-Peer Influence

Samuel Mills and the others took every opportunity to encourage their friends to think about global mission endeavors and to show them its basis in the Scripture. It is students, more than staff and pastors, calling upon one another to be message bearers that will exponentially increase the numbers of those who go out.

3. The Place of Faith

Who knows what God might do through the serious and devoted prayers of His people? Did Mills and the others know that their actions would have historic scope? Did they have any idea of the outcomes and the momentum of their ideas, prayers and actions? Of course not! They were just five ordinary guys committed to an extraordinary God. They asked Him to do the impossible and He answered them. It is the same today. Who knows what ministries and works of God might be birthed as a result of the heartfelt actions of the emerging generation.

4. It Doesn't Take Many

The final key principle to integrate into our lives is that it doesn't take many to bring about change. Movements commence by the faith and efforts of a few committed individuals. John Wesley once said, "Give me one hundred men and women who love nothing but God and hate nothing but sin and I'll change the world in the next twenty years." These must be willing to face opposition, however, and remain steadfast to the call.

ROBERT WILDER AND THE PRINCETON FOREIGN MISSIONARY SOCIETY

More than seventy years after the Haystack prayer meeting, an important individual came onto the scene. In 1881, Robert P. Wilder enrolled at Princeton College, where there had been some rumblings of message bearer interest. The Intercollegiate Movement had started there just a few years before, and it placed somewhat of a priority on challenging students to reach the world.

Wilder, at a mission meeting in Connecticut, heard A.J. Gordon preach a stirring message on the need to be filled with the Spirit to be effective in ministry.[xv] Gordon declared, "God is ready to give you the power of His Spirit as soon as you are ready to obey Him." This fired up young Wilder, and he and his fellow students returned to Princeton with a passion to awaken in others on campus a cross-cultural ministry interest.

In 1883, these students founded the Princeton Foreign Missionary Society for the strict purpose of calling young Christians to understand the heart of God for all humankind and the need to respond with action - specifically by going to the ends of the earth! Any student could join the group by subscribing to the following covenant,

"We, the undersigned, declare ourselves willing and desirous, God permitting, to go to the unevangelized portions of the world."[xvi]

In 1885-86, Wilder and his sister Grace met nightly to pray for the spread of this student mission movement to other colleges. They specifically asked God for 1,000 volunteers to go overseas as laborers.[xvii]

Principles For Today

1. Don't Waste Your College Years

Even though Wilder was a sickly young man, he used his college years to grow in God and leadership. This is our example today. Too many promising young believers are sidetracked by the lure of simply having fun in college and the lie that one can get serious about the things of God afterward. What a tremendous waste of a season that God intends to use for growth, teaching, and spiritual preparation for a lifetime of serving Him.

2. Momentum Is Powerful

A second key principle from Wilder's days in college is that momentum is powerful. Wilder got people excited about serving God globally on Princeton's campus. People were signing the volunteer declaration and devoted prayer for the nations was taking place regularly. There was a spiritual sense of anticipation and excitement on the campus and spiritual momentum helped influence many of the students.

THE MOUNT
HERMON CONFERENCE

A month-long conference at Mt. Hermon, Massachusetts, during the summer of 1886 proved to be the place where God would move in response to many prayers. Luther Wishard, a young YMCA leader, had been reading of the Haystack Five whom God had used to propel North America's involvement in foreign mission. He traveled to the haystack monument on the Williams College campus which had been erected in 1854,[xviii] and asked God to use his generation to finish what the Haystack students had begun. Wishard was one of the leaders to encourage the great evangelist D.L Moody to hold the Mt. Hermon conference. Beginning on July 6, 1886, two hundred and fifty-one students from eighty-six colleges came together to sit under the teaching of Moody for one month. Moody focused primarily on subjects directly related to evangelism.

The conference lacked any formal structure and no global mission emphasis was included in the program by the organizers.[xix] Wilder, however, was at the conference and this meant that God's global purpose would be highlighted! Before he left for the conference his sister Grace told him that she prophetically sensed that one hundred students would volunteer for missionary service at Mt. Hermon and that the Princeton Society would become an intercollegiate movement.

Two weeks went by without any public mention of global mission during any of the Mt. Hermon sessions. Wilder then approached Dr. A.T. Pierson, a leading advocate of global mission, and persuaded him to give a message on the subject for the conference. Pierson agreed and entitled his message, "All should go, and go to all"[xx] Following this address, Wilder became even more bold and went directly to Moody, asking if he could gather ten students to hold a session on the subject of the forgotten peoples of the world. Moody responded positively. John R. Mott, who would later become the first chairman of the Student Volunteer Movement, claimed the session, "did more to influence decisions than anything else that happened in those memorable days."[xxi] Wilder says of the session, known as the 'Meeting of Ten Nations', "Seldom have I seen an audience under the sway of God's Spirit as it was that night!"[xxii]

As the final two weeks went on, more of the messages surrounded the call to take the gospel to the ends of the earth. By the end of the conference, one hundred people had signed the Princeton Covenant committing themselves, "God permitting, to become foreign missionaries." These students became known as the "Mt. Hermon One Hundred", and are especially remarkable because global mission was never highlighted in the advertisements for the conference. Yet forty percent of the attendees left having committed their lives to go to the ends of the earth, during a time when a message bearer went for life![xxiii] At this time short-term mission trips did not exist, making the commitments of these college students all the more inspiring and remarkable.

When the conference concluded, there was a sense among many of the students that what had happened at Mount Hermon needed to be proclaimed on a wider scale. Wilder and another student decided to take the next school year off and tour college campuses in America and Canada sharing what had happened at Mt. Hermon. Their purpose was to challenge their peers with the vision of God's mission to the world, calling them to go to the nations upon graduation. They traveled to 162 institutions, an amazing accomplishment considering they traveled by train. After one year they had seen 2,106 students sign the volunteer declaration to become message bearers upon graduation.[xxiv]

Principles for Today

1. One Person Can Make a Difference

The influence of one single-minded and devoted person can change everything. Wilder was used of God to change the whole direction of the entire Mt. Hermon conference. Most often we feel as if our contribution means nothing, so we don't step out in faith and try. If God moves in today's emerging generation, it will be as a result of those who will take Him at His word, and step out as one single-minded and devoted person.

2. The Bible Can Be Trusted to Impact

If we become those who are committed to the word of God and who use it to challenge others, we will see fruit. The students who traveled the country telling others about what happened at Mt. Hermon used the truth of the Scriptures to call their peers to global ministry involvement. These responded to the Biblical exhortation as they sensed the Holy Spirit calling them as message bearers upon graduation.

THE STUDENT VOLUNTEER MOVEMENT

On December 6, 1888, the Student Volunteer Movement (SVM) was officially founded, and John R. Mott was elected as Chairman of the Executive Committee – a post he held for the next thirty-two years. Between 1891 and 1910 the movement experienced phenomenal growth under his leadership, as multitudes of students were mobilized into mission commitment on campuses all over the nation. Mott wrote, "At one time before the war (WWI) the number [of volunteers] in such circles exceeded 40,000 in 700 institutions." [xxv]

One of the most profound elements God used among the students was the watchword adopted by the movement: "The evangelization of the world in this generation." Mott said, "I can truthfully answer that next to the decision to take Christ as leader and Lord of my life, the watchword has had more influence to widen my horizon and enlarge my conception of the kingdom of God than all other ideals and objectives combined".[xxvi] The Spirit of God had infused these students' hearts with a firm faith to believe that the gospel could go around the world and touch all humanity in their lifetime.

The SVM began to lose steam during World War I, and by 1920 the "great change" had occurred in the theological presuppositions upon which the SVM had been founded and built. During the SVM conferences after 1920, many delegates became more concerned with the various post-WWI social issues in America than with God's global purposes.

Principles for Today

1. Waiting for Something to Give Our Lives For

The power of the SVM was its challenge to God's global purpose as fruit of true discipleship. People responded in droves because it demanded their all. Today the emerging generation is similarly waiting to respond to something that demands their all. We have coddled and played games with them instead of calling them and training them as the spiritual warriors God has ordained them to be.

2. The Emerging Generation Affects the Whole Church

The passion and commitment of those who went to the ends of the earth had a profound affect on the Church of their day, increasing its focus on global mission, including their fervent prayer for it and their financial giving to it. The commitment and vibrancy of the emerging generation plays an important part in helping the whole church to prioritize the fulfillment of the Great Commission.

ANOTHER WAVE ROLLS IN

In the 1920s and 1930s, the advance of God's Kingdom worldwide was inhibited – the Great Depression substantially reduced giving, and rationalism was severely dismantling theology. Yet in this apparent darkness, God worked to rekindle students' hearts for his global plan.

On a Thursday morning in February of 1936, on the Wheaton College (Illinois) campus, a male student stood as the chapel service was coming to a close and asked loudly what Christian students who truly love the Lord should do to receive the fullness of the Holy Spirit's power. He had a concern that too many of his fellow students walked in a fear of emotionalism, which hindered the work of the Holy Spirit[xxvii]. Many students responded, and the service turned into a time of repentance and seeking God for forgiveness and power from the Holy Spirit that lasted until the evening hours.

Robert C. McQuilkin, founding President of Columbia Bible College in South Carolina, was slated as the chapel speaker that morning, but due to illness, he did not bring a message. After this outbreak of repentance, however, McQuilkin decided to stay on the campus for an extra week. The next day he got a chance to speak, and brought a message with a focus on taking the gospel to the ends of the earth. In this revival atmosphere of the following week, many students stood and made personal commitments to involvement in global, cross-cultural ministry upon their graduation[xxviii].

THE STUDENT
FOREIGN MISSIONS FELLOWSHIP

In June of that same year, fifty-three students from a variety of college campuses met in North Carolina with Dr. McQuilkin to discuss their responsibility for the world. Great concern was expressed for the lack of cross-cultural ministry emphasis on campuses around the country. In Dr. McQuilkin, the students found a man of God who encouraged and advised them on how to revive message bearer interest in the colleges of the day.

From this gathering was formed a committee to consider starting a new movement "That would dedicate itself to the awakening of missionary interest among students." These students, plus others from the Keswick student conferences, helped to lay the groundwork for the Student Foreign Missions Fellowship (SFMF), which would touch thousands of lives on behalf of overseas missions. The stated purpose of the SFMF was, "...to stir the Church to the pressing obligation to make Christ known in all the world[xxix]."

In 1941 the Inter-Varsity Christian Fellowship movement was gaining momentum and crossed the Canada / U.S. border for the first time, beginning a chapter at the University of Michigan. IVCF at that time did not have a focus on global mission. Leaders from the SFMF and IVCF met and discussed a merger in early 1946 to form an incredibly multi-faceted movement[xxx]. J. Christy Wilson, who would later have a long and fruitful ministry in Afghanistan, was appointed the Missionary Secretary of the conglomerate in 1946.

THE BEGINNINGS OF URBANA

There was a great impact in the development of message bearer vision on campuses in the early months of the merger in 1946 – so much so that Wilson planned for a student missionary conference similar to what had taken place in the early days of the SVM. His concept was simple. He said, "The future of the evangelical student missionary outreach would be realized only if evangelical students discovered one another in their Lord." [xxxi]

Much, however, stood in the way of Wilson's vision. The IVCF/SFMF statement of faith was not well-received by the academic world, and many institutions did not want to host the conference. The organization placed the Bible as their authority for life and faith, and this did not sit well in the mid-40s academic climate. Wilson was persistent, however, and finally the University of Toronto welcomed the group to hold the first post-WWII student missionary convention from December 27, 1946 – January 1, 1947. Five hundred and seventy-five student delegates packed the facilities that held only 500.

As a result of the convention, forty IVCF chapters were set up in six months around the country, and many of these emphasized solid cross-cultural ministry vision. Interest in holding another student mission convention arose quickly, this time on American soil. Many universities were contacted, and again, most refused to allow the convention to use their campus. Finally an agreement was reached with the University of Illinois at Urbana, and the second SFMF/IVCF International Missionary Conference took place in 1948 with more than 1300 students in attendance[xxxii].

THE LAST 50 YEARS

During the second half of the twentieth century, several important ministries and revival movements came onto the scene that would play an important role in stirring the emerging generation toward involvement in the Great Commission. Campus Crusade for Christ was founded by Bill Bright in 1951 on the campus of UCLA. Operation Mobilization (OM) traces its history to a woman in the Unites States in the 1950s who prayed that God would save high school students where she lived and send them out as message bearers. George Verwer gave his life to Christ after receiving a gospel of John from this woman. In 1957 OM was initiated with a literature distribution outreach to Mexico. Loren Cunningham launched Youth With a Mission (YWAM) in 1960 from southern California after the Lord gave him a vision of waves of young people crashing onto the shores of every continent and being involved in aggressive evangelism. The 1970s brought the Jesus Movement, with thousands of counter-cultural young people giving their lives to Christ. Many sensed the call of God to cross-cultural ministry and went to serve the Lord in various areas of the world.

In 1980 a new expression of the student mission movement came into being. On the campus of Penn State University, some students decided to plan for and host a Student Conference on World Evangelization (SCOWE). On February 2 of that year, the event took place with Greg Livingstone (founder of Frontiers), Ralph Winter (founder of the US Center for World Mission) and Jay Gary[xxxiii] as speakers. About 500 students participated in this day-long conference and several responded to the speakers making commitments to go to the hard places in the world as message bearers.

Many students were stirred by this conference, and devoted themselves to continue to pray for one another to remain strong and vigilant in their commitments, as well as to ask God to move powerfully among the nations. In March 1980 one student shared at a prayer meeting his discovery of the Old Testament character, Caleb. Caleb's zeal in following the Lord wholeheartedly against great odds reflected these students' desire, so they called their committed little group Caleb Project.

The following year four young men who had responded at the SCOWE and made commitments to go to hard places, went to Libya as English teachers. Libya was probably the most "closed" country at that time. Each young man came home after about a year invigorated to call others to similar ventures.

Caleb Project developed an accountability structure to follow up those who signed the Caleb Declaration, a card signifying commitment to reaching the world for Christ. This small initiative continued to grow as more students signed the Declaration and were inducted into an innovative community, seeking to serve the Church with resources to help stir and develop mission vision.

Also in the 1980s the GO Conference was gaining momentum. This was a student-led conference focused on cultivating mission vision that took place every few years in the southeastern U.S.. God used this conference to impact multitudes of students, many of whom are today serving in very difficult regions of the world.

What a powerful history we have in the student mission movement! The stories shared are but the tip of the iceberg as there have been several other initiatives from many different countries that God has also used. It is critical to know our history as we move forward in this timely hour.

[i]   Pete Greig, *Awakening Cry* (London, England: Silver Fish Publishing, 1998) p. 134

[ii]   Howard Taylor, Hudson Taylor's Spiritual Secret.

[iii]   Bruce Olson, Bruchko

[iv]   Winkie Pratney, *Fire On The Horizon* (Ventura, CA: Renew Books, 1999) p. 113

[v]   Paul Pierson, *Lecture Notes – Historical Development of the Christian Movement* (Fuller Theological Seminary – Individual Distance Learning) p. 60

[vi]   Pete Greig, p. 40

[vii]   Greg Livingstone, p. 51

[viii]   Wilbert Norton, *To Stir The Church* (Madison, WI: 1986) p.2

[ix]   Ibid, p.2

[x]   Ralph D. Winter, *Four Men, Three Eras* – Article (Pasadena, CA: US Center For World Mission – William Carey Library) - http://www.uscwm.org/mobilization_division/resources/web_articles_11-20- 01/4_men_3_eras/4_men_3_eras.html

[xi]   David Howard, *Student Power In World Evangelism* (Downers Grove, IL: Inter-Varsity Press, 1970) p.75

[xii]   Ibid, p. 81

[xiii]   Ibid, p. 82

[xiv]   Ibid, p. 77

[xv]   Ibid, p.76

[xvi]   Timothy Wallstrom, *The Creation of a Student Movement To Evangelize The World* (Pasadena, CA: William Carey Publishing, 1980) p. 35

[xvii]   David Howard, p. 87

[xviii]   This is the only monument in church history erected to a prayer meeting and it still stands today on the Williams College campus in Williamstown, Massachusetts.

[xix]   Ibid, p. 42

[xx]   Ibid, p. 43

[xxi]   Ibid, p. 44

[xxii]   Ibid, p. 44

[xxiii]   Ibid p. 44

[xxiv]   David Howard, p. 92

xxv Ibid, p. 97

xxvi Ibid, p.87

xxvii Wilbert Norton, p.7

xxviii Ibid, p.8

xxix Ibid, p.20

xxx David Howard, p.99

xxxi Wilbert Norton, p.31

xxxii Ibid, p.34

xxxiii Greg Fritz, *History of Caleb Project* (unpublished paper) p.1

Then the word of the Lord came to me, saying

"Before I formed you in the womb I knew you;

before you were born I sanctified you:

ordained you a prophet to the nations.

Then said I, "Ah, Lord God!

Behold I cannot speak, for I am a youth."

But the Lord said to me:

"Do not say, 'I am a youth,'

for you shall go to all to whom I send you,

and whatever I command you, you shall speak.

Do not be afraid of their faces,

for I am with you to deliver you," says the Lord.

JEREMIAH 1:4-8

"TELL THE STUDENTS TO GIVE UP THEIR SMALL
AMBITIONS AND COME EASTWARD TO PREACH THE
GOSPEL OF CHRIST."
Francis Xavier

CHAPTER 4

SIX TRENDS IN THE STUDENT MISSION WORLD

There are six primary trends in the student mission world that are important to understand. They help us gauge what to do next as we move in the direction of a renewed and thriving student mission movement today. For if we don't know what's taking place, or possibly more importantly what's not taking place, we cannot rightly discern how to waken the giant and participate with God in the resurging student mission movement.

1. The Short-Term Myth

In his book, *The Missions Addiction*, David Shibley shares that, "there were more American teenagers on mission trips last summer [2000] than ever in the history of this nation."[i] While the number of young adults involved in short-term cross-cultural ministry (two weeks to six months) today is staggering, the number of new long-term workers, from the emerging generation, continues to dwindle![ii]

Although nearly half of young adults return from a short-term trip with an initial excitement about possible long-term involvement, very few ever make it overseas. "I'd guess that between ten and twenty percent consider long-term commitment, but none from my group are now overseas,"[iii] said a campus ministry leader in California. One-third of students never give a thought to future long-term involvement after a short-term trip. A campus ministry leader in New York admitted, "None of my students have come back and considered vocational missions."

It seems that we are in the midst of a disturbing and subtle reality in short-term mission understanding. Could it be that short-term participation is not translating into long-term global mission involvement because the reasons for going on the short-term trip have become skewed?

The original intent of the first short-term trips in the 1960s was for potential long-term workers to survey the place in the world that they sensed God calling them to go as laborers. By contrast, as a denominational representative in California stated, "Short-term trips these days appear to highlight having a 'spiritual experience' rather than producing prepared laborers for the global harvest."

A related dilemma is that many students perceive involvement in global mission as synonymous with short-term or a summer trip. Students may come home from a summer or spring break trip and check "missions" off their spiritual checklist of things to do – they have gone on a summer or spring break trip to serve Jesus and have completed their "missions" responsibility. Now they can finish college, get a job, and do their own thing, all because they participated in a two-week summer mission trip.

In many cases, short-term trips have become just another part of the Church's curriculum for the emerging generation. The need and purpose of the Kingdom of God being planted globally by long-term workers is usually not discussed, certainly not in a way that personalizes the message, and causes an individual to consider the role that they can play in reaching the forgotten around the world for Christ.

2. The Missing Long-Term Challenge

Not only is short-term activity all too present today, but there is a simultaneous absence of a long-term challenge in the student world in America. Only eight percent of mission speakers challenge college-aged young adults to consider long-term, cross-cultural ministry overseas when they graduate.[iv] A leader of a large campus ministry in California admitted, "I'm trying to remember... I honestly can't recall the last time I heard a call to long-term mission involvement." Can the Church expect a solid long-term return on eight percent of mission speakers putting a long-term challenge before the emerging generation? Usually mission speakers tell stories from around the world and challenge students to take a short-term trip, but neglect to mention serving Jesus long-term around the world.

We need to see the glory and honor of God declared throughout the earth. Who will devote their lives to sowing the gospel among forgotten peoples around the world? It is clear that short-term activity will not suffice to meet this end. Without a radical shift in focus and a significant increase in the long-term challenge presented to the emerging generation, the completion of the Great Commission in our day is an elusive dream.

I here define long-term ministry as a minimum of two years of cross-cultural service. Sadly, the opportunity to spend at least two years serving Jesus in places where the least access to the gospel exists appears not to cross the mind of the average Christian young adult. This is primarily because they haven't been given a relevant vision for it.

Recently I spoke to a group of college students and challenged them to commit themselves to going to a difficult, Islamic nation, for at least two years after graduation. A young man doing a one-year Bible school course rushed up to my wife after the meeting and asked, "How do I do this?" Kelly began to ask questions to gauge where he was at and asked, "Well, do you have any experience overseas?" He responded with "No, but I just know that God is calling me to give my life to this stuff!" We rejoiced that this young man caught the vision of a whole life set apart for God's global purpose.

A minimum of two years gives the opportunity for message bearers to learn the language, grasp cultural issues, and develop meaningful relationships through which to share the gospel. It also provides a long enough amount of time to hit the wall of culture shock, and persevere through the temptation of wanting to leave and get back to what is familiar as quickly as possible.

In reality, however, this amount of time is not long enough to see enduring fruit in most least-reached areas. Thus, the challenge made to students by a growing number of leaders and ministries is to go for at least two years, believing that through serving God globally for at least this amount of time, many will find themselves unable to come back home for good, and as a result will commit themselves afresh for the long-term. This challenge is a first step in a lifelong call of following Jesus to the ends of the earth.

3. Global Mission Emphasis in the Student World

Close to half of college ministries in the United States emphasize global mission by promoting or hosting sporadic events throughout the year, often dedicating one meeting each semester to discuss missions.[v] Most commonly, this includes a sharing time where young adults who went on short-term trips during the previous summer get to share their experiences. Is this enough to provide ample vision and understanding of the biblical motivation for global ministry?

Some leaders are using creative means to give students global vision. One such leader oversees a region of campus ministry fellowships in California, and began a "Dead Missionary Society" for some of the men in his discipleship group. Patterned after the movie "Dead Poet's Society", he goes the whole nine yards with it. They meet periodically in a cave near the school, have snacks and read aloud the adventures and writings of message bearers who wrote about their lives in God's harvest fields.

One-third of college ministries have no global mission emphasis whatsoever, as understandably, campus evangelism and discipleship are the primary focal points of most campus ministries and church college ministries.![vi] A leader of a campus ministry in Massachusetts said, "We have so much that we have to be about. Our organizations have many facets that they want us to focus on and we can't give all things the same attention, thus global mission can get relegated to a side show!"

When a campus ministry leader in New York spoke to me about the mission emphasis in his fellowship, he forcefully replied that, "Campus evangelism is missions." Shall our definition of mission be so broad? As many of my professors at Fuller are fond of saying, "If everything we do is mission, then nothing is mission."

Reaching out on campuses to fellow students who do not yet know the love of Jesus Christ is accomplishing what Jesus came to do – to seek and save the lost. Yet the Great Commission includes not only Jerusalem or one's hometown, but also Judea, Samaria, and the ends of the earth. Charles Van Engen of Fuller Seminary says: "Mission is the people of God intentionally crossing cultural barriers from church to non-church, faith to non-faith to proclaim by word and deed the coming of the Kingdom of God in Jesus Christ."[vii]

In no way does this minimize the incredible needs on college campuses in areas where the gospel is plentiful. In America, the Church growth rate of 2.2 million annually has been slightly below the population growth rate of 2.6 million annually. The growing diversity of types of people and the compartmentalization of North American culture makes evangelism increasingly difficult.[viii]

Pastor Larry Stockstill says, "People in the United States who are not born again are unsaved, but they are probably not unreached." Churches in which the Word of God is faithfully preached can be found in every town and city across the U.S. as well as other parts of the world including the United Kingdom, Canada, Sub-Saharan Africa, parts of southern India, and many other countries. As well as churches, there are Christian television and radio shows that constantly broadcast Christian messages. By contrast, those born in the 10/40 window and some places in the 40/70 window (primarily Western Europe) could conceivably live their entire lives with no viable access to the gospel message.

4. A Renewed Call to Sacrifice

Some who work among the emerging generation communicate a lack of confidence in the commitment level of today's average young adult, saying that because the emerging generation struggles to make responsible choices and remain dedicated, we must be cautious in encouraging them to participate in challenging endeavors.

On the other hand, most workers feel that instead of catering to this cultural inheritance of non-commitment, we should issue a renewed call to absolute sacrifice and obedience to God.[x] According to a campus leader in Connecticut, "John Piper's call to sacrifice today is desperately needed. This appeals to students. Deep down every person desires to believe something so deeply they are willing to suffer for it." A campus ministry leader in Nigeria agreed as he commented, "Students today seem more willing to count the cost to see the gospel taken across cultures."

In the movie *Pearl Harbor*, the main character is asked by a British officer why he is so anxious to fight, and possibly die in, another country's battle. The character responds matter-of-factly that he's "Not anxious to die, just anxious to matter!" This is a powerful commentary on today's emerging generation.

I firmly believe that as the bar is raised, the emerging generation will respond wholeheartedly. One hundred years ago, John R. Mott said, "I have never been disappointed when I've heaped tremendous responsibility upon a young person." William Carey, the father of modern global missions, challenged his generation to "Attempt great things for God and expect great things from God."[xi] This is a timely appeal – this generation deserves to be given a big vision of a big God who isn't afraid of the various idiosyncrasies of our world!

It is critical to allow the Holy Spirit to shift our paradigms of sacrifice. We, specifically in the western church, don't have much understanding of Biblical suffering. Tragically, many of our teachings tell us that something is terribly wrong if we are suffering. A simple, honest study of suffering in the New Testament reveals that early Christians faced suffering and believed that it was a part of the life of a follower of Jesus (Philippians 3:10).

Most non-western cultures have a deeper understanding and experience of suffering. In Romania, for example, many believers in the church have learned courage and strength by enduring the previous communist regime, potentially preparing young Romanians for work among the forgotten.

In *Let the Nations Be Glad*, John Piper says, "Some suffering is the calling of every believer, but especially of those that God calls to bear the gospel to the unreached."[xii] Deitrich Bonhoeffer's famous lines are absolutely biblical and demand our consideration. "The cross is not the terrible end to an otherwise God-fearing and happy life, but it meets us at the beginning of our communion with Christ. When Christ calls a man, he bids him come and die." [xiii]

Envision a generation that truly internalizes the command to take up the cross and die daily, living out the reality of being crucified with Christ (Galatians 2:20) and of not being "our own": *"And you are not your own. For you were bought at a price; therefore glorify God in your body and in your spirit, which are God's"*(1 Corinthians 6:19-20). As children of God, cleansed and washed by the blood of Jesus, we no longer have any rights, nor do we belong to ourselves, but to Him to be used as His vessels for His purposes alone.

5. Peer-on-Peer Influence

In the emerging generation a tendency is evident surrounding young adults responding best when they are challenged by one another. Today twenty-two percent of students in college ministries exhort others to think about "missions-type" things.[xiv] A campus ministry leader in Massachusetts gives an example of a student exhortation that extended beyond being involved in short-term mission trips. "One student recently addressed the group and talked about what a shameful thing it was that we don't have more 'missions' vision."

In Singapore, a movement called Joshua 21 is seeing fruit among students. It is a cooperative movement among various churches and organizations that challenges the emerging generation with prayer and mission vision. Many students are challenging their fellow peers at the large gatherings. In Manila, Philippines, students are taking responsibility to lead their fellow students like never before. In this country where seventy-five percent of the entire population is under thirty years old, leaders say that the emerging generation has the potential to lead the way in involvement in the Great Commission. Every generation which has seen a genuine student mission awakening has had radical student leaders promoting God's global vision in their midst.

The students involved in the original Student Volunteer Movement, affectionately known as volunteers, had a two-pronged agenda during their college years. The first point was to prepare for the country they would sail to upon graduation. This meant language acquisition, cultural study, and a host of other preparations. The second was to be communicators of global mission vision among their Christian peers on their campuses and in their churches.[xv] They were gripped with the global purpose of God, and it was manifested as they gathered students together for prayer gatherings saturating the needs of the world in prayer, informational meetings discussing the needs and opportunities, and deep study of the Scriptures to understand God's plan for the world and His call for their involvement. Imagine this impassioned community life making its way into cafeterias, student unions, dorms, and apartments of universities around the world. It's beginning to happen and will only increase in the coming days as the giant is wakened!

6. What's Happening Through Worship?

Something significant has been taking place over the past decade in the realm of corporate worship. As seen in any college-aged worship gathering, the emerging generation is clearly at the forefront of this revival of worship. Can we say then that something of extraordinary proportions is happening among the emerging generation through these gatherings?

Do we find a correlation between worship and the formation of deeper character as evidenced in a greater passion for Jesus and for those who are lost apart from Him? The following are observations of possible trends as it is difficult to draw conclusions on this subject. God alone knows the hearts and minds of those in the emerging generation – the fears and insecurities, and what scars are being hidden due to varied painful experiences.

More than half of college leaders note that present worship is very "me-oriented", meaning that the lyrics focus on Jesus and me (relationship songs).[xvi] It tends to leave out the depth of greatness of His attributes, His call to love others and His devotion to the whole world. Generally there is not an increase in compassion for the lost or an increase in the character of students that could be connected to the increased intensity of the worship.[xvii]

"Too many young adults are seeking an encounter with God instead of seeking to be in line with His heart and to do His will," remarked a mission leader in California. Another national campus ministry leader in Wisconsin noticed, "Students seem to have a wonderfully intimate experience with God during the meetings and then go back into their life and get busied."

Thirty-two percent of leaders say that fruit is slow in coming, but they know students are falling deeper in love with Jesus through the avenue of worship. "The worship revival we're seeing shows this generation's hunger for God. Unfortunately there are some cultural things that are involved in it as well," commented a campus pastor of a Christian university in California. One leader of a Texas campus ministry commented positively, "There is an emotional shallowness to their lives [young adults] and during worship they really touch God at an emotional level."

No matter how it is described, there is something taking place in these worship meetings in which young adults are focusing on Jesus. It seems God has been highlighting something fundamental through this revival of worship.[xviii] He is reminding His body of the Great Commandment that must take precedence in our hearts as we work towards the fulfillment of the Great Commission. We must have our priorities in the proper order, as He is more jealous for our devotion than He is the work we do for Him.

The Great Commandment is the source of all true ministry. *"You shall love the Lord your God with all your heart, with all your soul, and with all your mind."*(Matthew 22:37) As we love Him completely and fully we will grow in our commitment to obey Him out of pure hearts and motives. Through the intensity of worship, many are kindling the fires with their First Love.

Isaiah 6:1-8 could be a picture of what is taking place. Isaiah's experience of and response to the glory of God paints for us a picture of the emerging generation. The passage can be divided into three distinct phases. The first phase (verses 1-2) is God's revelation of His glory to Isaiah. The second phase (verses 3-7) is the revelation of God's holiness that brings on true repentance. The third phase (verse 8) concludes with God conversing with the rest of the Trinity and asking the question, "Whom shall I send and who will go for Us?"

Isaiah, his heart having been prepared by the first two revelations of God's glory and His holiness, hears the message bearer call and commits to it immediately. His heart and will had been prepared by the Lord, enabling him to answer God's call to go.

It appears that the emerging generation is presently in the first phase. God is giving many a glimpse of His glory, drawing them to fall more deeply in love with Him. Their hunger for intimacy with Jesus is growing through worship. Their intimacy is not yet turning into intensified evangelism and prayer, but if we take Isaiah's experience as a model, these will soon follow.[xix]

God desires to bathe His people with His presence to make them ready for the revelation of His holiness that will convict us of impurity as we see God for Who He is and our hearts are grieved to the core as we see the sickness of our sin. Yet in His glorious mercy, He cleanses us from all sin, shame, and guilt and renews us. Then we will be able and available to receive the privilege of responding to His message bearer challenge with the beautifully surrendered and abandoned words, "Here am I, send me!"

RESPONDING TO THE TRENDS

I believe that these trends in today's student mission world suggest that we have been and are missing the mark. This is the very defini- tion of "sin" – to miss the mark. On our Christian campuses, in our local churches, and in our campus ministry organizations we've let the global heart cry of Jesus be pushed to the side as second-rate. It is not enough to recognize the trends for purely scientific or research- based purposes to help us know what to do next; we must own them as sin and embrace a heart of deep repentance in view of such prevailing realities. A. W. Tozer said, "The truest and most acceptable repentance is to reverse the acts and attitudes of which we repent."[xx] We must cry out to God from the very core of our hearts in repentance for not taking His purposes in the world seriously. We have not allowed the Holy Spirit to use us in global, cross-cultural ministry, and in doing so we have grieved Him immensely. I encourage us to take a moment to search our own hearts and ask the Holy Spirit to show us how we have missed the mark and seek to practically "reverse the acts and attitudes" which He might show us.

These trends help us to isolate holes that must be filled to see the effective rebuilding of the student mission movement today. As we continue, we will explore four building blocks for the global resurgance of the movement on campuses and in churches. We must grasp and determine to implement these on campuses if we are going to move ahead and see the trends mentioned in this chapter changed and righted.

---

i   David Shibley, The Missions Addiction (Lake Mary, Fl: Charisma House, 2001) p. 56

ii   Ryan Shaw, This Generation For The Forgotten (Unpublished Compilation of Campus Research Findings) p. 19

iii   Ibid, p. 19

iv   Ibid, p.22

v   Ibid, p. 16

vi   Ibid, p. 17

vii   Charles Van Engen, Course Reader for MT542 at Fuller Seminary, cover page

viii   David Shibley, p. 139

ix   Ibid, p. 139

x   Ryan Shaw, p. 25

xi   Website - http://home.snu.edu/~hculbert/slogans.htm

xii   John Piper, Let The Nations Be Glad (Grand Rapids, MI: Baker Books, 1993) p. 78

xiii   Deitrich Bonhoeffer, The Cost Of Discipleship (New York: The McMillan Co., 1963) p. 99

xiv   Ryan Shaw, p.27

xv   Timothy Wallstrom, p.58

xvi   Ryan Shaw, p.31

xvii   Ibid, p.76

xviii   Ibid, p.31

xix   Ibid, p.76

xx   A.W. Tozer, The Divine Conquest (Camp Hill, PA; Christian Publications, 1950) p. 75

Then to Him was given dominion

and glory and a kingdom,

that all peoples, nations and languages

should serve Him.

His dominion is an everlasting dominion,

which shall not pass away,

and His kingdom the one

which shall never be destroyed.

DANIEL 7:14

"FOR THE FIRST TIME IN HISTORY, THE TOTAL
EVANGELIZATION OF THIS PLANET IS MORE THEN A PIPE
DREAM. TRUE, THE POPULATION IS LARGER THEN EVER.
THE OPPOSITION IS STRONGER THEN EVER. YET THE
RESOURCES TO FINISH THE JOB ARE GREATER THEN EVER."

David Shibley

CHAPTER 5

BUILDING BLOCKS FOR TODAY'S MOVEMENT

One of the greatest hindrances to the advancement of the Kingdom of God around the world has been a lack of individual believers personally owning this responsibility. This has been because of a variety of excuses, misunderstandings of the heart of God and Scriptural ignorance. William Carey believed that God intended every believer to play a role in the cross-cultural mission of the Church. His reading of Scripture convinced him that all were called to go unless God clearly led them to stay.[i] Jesus Christ is the originator and leader of His global, Kingdom work. Those who walk with Him and abide in Him will be ready to know and to do His will. The great South African pastor, Andrew Murray writes, "It is simply a matter of being near enough to Him to hear His voice, and so devoted to Him and His love as to be ready to do His will."[ii]

This may seem like an oversimplification, in view of the complicated realities in our world today, so let's break it down. Scripture makes it clear that we have been justified through faith in Jesus Christ primarily for the purpose of having a restored relationship with God the Father and to enjoy relationship with Him immensely. Secondly, it is for the purpose of being the witnesses of Christ's love, partnering with Him in manifesting the breaking in of the Kingdom of God on this earth. To prepare us for such a calling, God has loved us and shed His love abroad in our hearts (Romans 5:5) and made His power available to us. In the same exact way that He loves us and wants relationship with us, He loves and wants relationship with those around the world who are outside of a relevant hearing of His love and what it can mean for them. The Bible tells us in 2 Peter 3:9 that, "... *The Lord is not willing that any should perish but that all should come to repentance!*" His desire is that those of us who have had such an amazing and undeserved opportunity to know this love would reveal it to those who have not. This is the greatest privilege of a follower of Jesus, and brings with it the highest joy, happiness, satisfaction and fulfillment.

Through relationship with Christ, His body is activated to accomplish His work. Andrew Murray writes, "Every member has only one objective, and while healthy, is every moment fulfilling that objective – to carry out the work of the Head. The work of our Head in heaven is to gather all the members of His body on earth. In this work every member of the body cooperates; not under the law of a blind force of nature, but under the law of the Spirit of life, which connects every believer with his Lord in love and imparts to him the same disposition and the same strength in which Christ does His work."[iii]

The All-Consuming Theme of the Bible

Because God's central desire is to restore fallen humanity to relationship with Himself, the theme of redemption is the focal point of the entire Bible, and the foundation of our personal visions of involvement in reaching the world for Christ. Henrietta Mears, the renowned Bible teacher and mentor of Billy Graham, the great evangelist, and Bill Bright, the founder of Campus Crusade for Christ, tells us, "The Bible has one main theme, Redemption, and many sub-themes that run through the entire book. Redemption is hinted at in the beginning (Genesis 3:15) and developed as the main theme, coming to the climax with the advent of Christ. The sub-themes, interwoven into the narrative and all dependent upon the main theme of redemption, are all defined and illustrated in the events of the Bible."[iv]

The Bible is the story of God's complete and all-consuming commitment throughout history to redeem humanity back into the relationship He originally enjoyed with them. When Adam sinned in Genesis 3, all humankind throughout all of history lost relationship with God and became steeped and caught in the bondage of sin. God accomplished this redemption once and for all by sending His own Son as the perfectly sinless (and thus the only available) sacrifice to take away the sin of humankind. Upon realizing the depth of His great sacrifice, repenting of our sinful nature, and believing with our hearts in the work of His Son, the way is opened for us to enjoy fellowship and potentially deep and intimate relationship with God, which was His intent from the beginning of time.

It is His ultimate and supreme purpose to see this redemption offered to every creature in every generation in a way that each can culturally understand and respond to. This story has stretched throughout history and continues today as each one of us chooses to take this story to the uttermost parts of the earth. If we are to faithfully and obediently walk in the ways and the will of God, we know that being a bearer of this message to all humanity is not optional.

How then can we be involved in this central purpose of the Father? God invites our participation in four primary ways, each of which is essential to creating environments in our campus communities where a contagious influence to see the forgotten reached can be realized. As Bible-believing followers of Jesus, all of us are called upon to do at least one of these, while most of us will do at least two, and many will take part in three or all four. To see millions of people genuinely turning to Christ and persevering in their faith, in the least-reached and most resistant cities and areas across the earth, we need all hands on deck, everyone in their ordained role, working together. These roles are (1) extravagant giving, (2) extraordinary praying, (3) surrendered going, and (4) impassioned mobilizing.

BUILDING BLOCK # 1 - EXTRAVAGANT GIVING

The Bible teaches that people are not the source for fulfilling any of our needs, but that God alone is to hold this place of provider in our hearts. It also teaches that He is the one that owns the cattle on a thousand hills (Psalm 50:10) and that all the gold and silver in the world is His (Haggai 2:8). If everyone who currently gives toward the Great Commission ceased their giving, we know that God would supernaturally provide for His work to continue. He provided food for Elijah through a raven (1 Kings 17:3-4). He caused the oil in the barrel to continue for the widow that Elijah met (1 Kings 17:13-16). He met the physical needs of 5,000 men and an equal number of women and children when Jesus supernaturally fed them with just a couple loaves of bread and two fish (John 6:10-14). God is able and He is faithful!

God Partners With Us

Having said this, we also know that God uses His children who willingly and cheerfully seek to obey Him to help finance the work of the global harvest (2 Corinthians 9:7). This opportunity brings with it deep joy and satisfaction. The stories, however, of workers who have been forced to leave their ministries around the world and come home because of a lack of funding are surprisingly numerous. It is a travesty and a black mark on the people of God that goers are hindered in their work because another part of the body- givers are not performing well their function; this grieves the very heart of God.

Members of the global Church earn an annual 12,300 billion U.S. dollars. 1.73% of this total income or 213 billion US dollars is given by these church members for Christian causes. Of this amount only 5.4% (11.4 billion U.S. dollars) of total giving among the entire global Church goes toward cross-cultural outreach (foreign mission activities) and church planting. Of this amount, only one percent goes to those working in forgotten areas where there is no established witness for Jesus.' Most of the funds for cross-cultural ministry are going to areas where the gospel is already planted.

It is true that God is able to provide, but He also is committed to partnering with a generation who will catch His global heartbeat and give extravagantly to see the Kingdom expanded among the forgotten. *"For the eyes of the Lord range throughout the earth to strengthen those whose hearts are fully committed to Him.(2 Chronicles 16:9)"*Are our hearts fully committed to the Lord?

The low status of current giving suggests that we do not really care about what He cares about. He is waiting for a wholehearted and devoted generation. The way we handle and steward the financial resources He has entrusted to us speaks volumes about our level of commitment and consecration to His purposes. We may need to rethink our priorities and align them with His purposes.

Blessed To Be a Blessing

One of the greatest thrills in a disciple's life is to participate in God's work through giving. Jesus told us that we cannot serve two masters (Matthew 6:24), but that we could choose either God or money as our master; it is not to control us, but we are to control it. We have been blessed financially not so that we can hoard money or spend it on ourselves, but so that we can be a blessing to others and to give to the worldwide harvest. As children of God, the same covenant that He made with Abraham in Genesis 12:2, applies to us; *"I will make you into a great nation and I will bless you; I will make your name great and you will be a blessing... And all peoples of earth will be blessed through you."*

The place to start is with the tithe. It is alarming to recognize how few believers actually tithe at least ten percent of their income to God. In Malachi 3:8-10 God rebukes Israel by declaring, *"Will a man rob God? Yet you rob me? But you ask 'How do we rob you?' 'In tithes and offerings. You are under a curse — the whole nation of you — because you are robbing me. Bring the whole tithe into the storehouse, that there may be food in my house. Test me in this,' says the Lord Almighty"*.

This is a serious rebuke; we are actually robbing God when we fail to give back to Him the first ten percent of all our income. This is the base level of Biblical giving and we needn't stop with this percentage. I know many who seek to incrementally increase the percentage of their giving annually. Several of these are now tithing well above thirty and even forty percent. Every dollar is His already, and by commanding us to tithe, He wants to teach us dependence on and confidence in Him, not our money.

One of the direst sins in many of our lives is greed. We always think that just a little more money will bring the fulfillment that we've always wanted. Greed in the Church today is hindering the global expansion of Christ's kingdom. We must counter this spirit of greed by learning, applying and teaching others this principle of generous giving early in our lives.

What if we lived the lifestyle of a radical giver throughout college and graduated having built a history of trusting God with our finances? As we watch Him provide for us in extraordinary ways, our hearts are filled with faith and trust. Worry and fear are defeated, and the number of people willing to continue to trust Him for their livelihood throughout their lives would increase exponentially. This can happen today as we challenge those in our spheres and ministries to trust the Lord with finances and give extravagantly to God and His global purpose. God calls us to this life of sacrificial giving, even before we can "afford" it. Remember that the dollar amount doesn't matter, but the heart of the giver is what God is after.

Reaping a Harvest through Giving

As we consecrate ourselves through our finances to the Lord, we reap a harvest related to the work being done around the world. We might not be doing the actual work, but we've entered into spiritual relationship with it through our giving, and thus receive a spiritual reward related to it. However, most of us are so busy keeping our checkbooks balanced that we don't step out and trust God by giving, even extravagantly, to His global works. I have often heard it said that we cannot out give God. What an amazing truth. If we give, He will take care of us. *"Do not be deceived, God is not mocked; for whatever a man sows, that he will also reap."*(Galatians 6:7).

Radicals Who Gave

Many students of the Volunteer Movement gave large amounts of money to friends who were sailing for the ends of the earth as message bearers. As these givers left college and got their first jobs, they had learned that God is faithful as they responded to His calling to give. They were able to continue trusting Him and some even committed to giving over sixty percent of their salaries to friends serving around the world as message bearers. They understood God's call to simplicity, and were willing to live on less than half of their income for the sake of giving to the global harvest.

I know one leader who has made it his aim to personally give away one million U.S. dollars to the global harvest before he dies. Today's emerging generation of believers seems to be extremely generous. A young man living in a colder climate in the U.S. came across a homeless man on the street one day wearing only a light windbreaker. With little thought he took off his hefty winter coat and gave it to this man. Leaders in Nigeria's student world have been surprised and encouraged by the willingness of their students to give and support mission work to the forgotten in West Africa. The desire to give is evident, so let's capitalize on it, calling the emerging generation to give extravagantly to the harvest that God is reaping around the world.

BUILDING BLOCK # 2 - EXTRAORDINARY PRAYING

As we assess the task of completing the Great Commission in our lifetime we know the only way that the ground in the most resistant areas to the gospel will be softened for the harvest is through the faithful, prophetic, and strategic intercessions of the Church. Paul writes in 2 Corinthians 4: 3-4, *"But even if our gospel is veiled, it is veiled to those who are perishing, whose minds the god of this age has blinded, who do not believe, lest the light of the gospel of the glory of Christ, who is the image of God, should shine on them."* It is evident through Scripture that one of the most important ministries of all is that of prayer and intercession. Apart from informed intercession focused on the forgotten of the world eyes will remain veiled by the god of this age, Satan. The emerging generation has the capacity to lead the way in restoring this kind of intercession in the believing collegiate communities of the world.

The days of boring prayer meetings must come to an end. Prayer meetings should be the most well-attended, vital, and exciting of all of our meetings. Prayer is our lifeline, and in order to see it and make use of it as such, many are heeding the need to reinvent the prayer meeting in our generation.⁵¹

It is prayer that has changed history. Communism was likely brought to its knees through the day and night intercession of the global Church, both from behind the Iron Curtain and in the west. If we are serious about seeing a breakthrough in the spiritual climate of our homes, campuses, cities, and among the forgotten peoples of the earth, we must become a people of creative, enthusiastic, and disciplined intercession. God loves it when we partner with Him in this capacity, giving ourselves to His call. It is time for prayer warriors to arise en masse and put their hands to the plow through this most valuable of ministries.

Are You Willing To Pay the Price?

In 1996, I worked as a janitor at my local church. The Lord used this job to show me deficiencies in my character, including pride. He also used it to teach me about prayer, the church building becoming my personal prayer closet. The work was mindless labor and afforded me the opportunity to spend each day drawing close to Him, worshipping, and crying out for others in intercession. I remember one day while I was vacuuming the sanctuary carpet, praying fervently and thinking highly of myself as a Christian because of my prayer life, when the Lord whispered in my ear, "Are you willing to pay the price?" I immediately repented of my pride and asked Him what this meant.

I knew there was a price to pay to know Him more deeply and to walk in spiritual power in prayer – something I wanted badly. But was I ready to pay the price to lay hold of it? I knew God was asking me to count the cost, recognizing that taking this road would not be easy. Would I continue to worship Him and seek His face and pray and intercede for others if I went through hardship and adversity? I timidly answered "yes" to Him, although I had no clue what this really meant.

God is not as concerned with our emotional responses to Him as He is with our faithfulness and devotion. Will we still be a people of prayer when the going gets tough? Will we pay the price by taking our eyes off of ourselves and deliberately keeping our hands dirty in the prayer closet? There is a cost to a powerful and effective lifestyle of intercession (James 5:16). It does not come easily. Many people talk about radical prayer but few actually do it effectively.

You Do Not Have Because You Do Not Ask!

It doesn't take much cross-cultural experience before the reality of our utter inability and inadequacy to produce spiritual fruit hits us square in the face. This is the place of humility and total dependence upon God that He seeks for us. It is in this place that we enter into the position of intercessor, knowing that only God can move the mountains that stand before the advancing Church.

All we have to do is ask. *"You do not have, because you do not ask!* (James 4:2)"* For many years, my immediate family prayed for the salvation of our relatives who were not yet followers of Jesus. We saw no fruit for years. Then a few years ago my aunt and cousin got connected with a local church in Phoenix and became believers. It was a radical change as they fully devoted themselves to Christ. My cousin began talking to her friends in her high school about Jesus, and there were lasting changes in her character and life. My uncle watched skeptically as these things unfolded. Coming from an engineering background, he wanted proof to put His faith in Jesus, but after awhile he could no longer deny the clear difference that had taken place in his wife and daughter. He gave his own life to Christ. Consistent prayer undoubtedly helped to unlock the doors of their hearts in the spiritual realm.

It is ridiculous to think that God's kingdom will advance even in small ways apart from asking, more asking, and even more asking. As we persist and remain consistent, we are like the widow in Jesus' parable in Luke 18 who day after day continued to ask the judge to give her justice. We know that in this parable Jesus was telling His followers to be vigilant and persistent in prayer as they approached the throne of God for breakthrough. Just as the judge finally conceded, God too will answer those who pray with this persistence. We must know, however, that it takes time and energy to entreat the Lord like this.

In many nations there are forgotten cities where message bearers have not been able to enter for years. This is a spiritual problem, not a practical one. The enemy, who does not want laborers to bring hope and love in the name of Jesus, has held shut the doors by manipulating the city authorities. However, we have been given the authority, through Jesus, to pray that the enemy's power will be broken over those authorities and that laborers will be welcomed with open arms into the city (Matthew 28:18). It is not just the responsibility of the workers to pray for this, but also the responsibility of the worldwide church to stand in the gap with power and to cry out to God for this sort of breakthrough among all peoples.

Prayer That Moves the Heart of God

God is after the prevailing, groaning prayer, even fasting, of our entire being – where praying His heart is our single focus and bringing His plans to fruition our top priority. The spiritual desires and yearnings of believers find their source in the Holy Spirit who dwells within our hearts, and He expresses them to God on our behalf with deep groans (Romans 8:26).

Many of us shy away from that which engages us at an emotional level, and this is to our detriment. God has created us as emotional beings, and He desires this part of us, as well as the rest of our being, to be captivated for His honor and purposes. What He doesn't want is for us to be dictated by our emotions or feelings, which can potentially deceive us. This can be a fine line to walk, but as we find ourselves devoting all of our being to God, He will move our emotions in the direction that they need to go. As we allow the Holy Spirit to lead us in the groaning we begin to "feel" His sorrow or joy or deep-seated compassion, rather than create our own to match what we perceive to be the need.

Jesus' Vision for His Church

It is Jesus' desire to get us to a point of fervent and uninterrupted prayer focused specifically on global harvest and revival. He says in Mark 11:17, *"Is it not written: 'My house will be called a house of prayer for all nations?'"* The Scripture tells us that He wants the church to become a place where prayer for all peoples, nations, and tongues is offered continually. About how many of our ministries or local churches can this be said? More often we put an emphasis on other items – preaching, announcements or special music – to the neglect of prayer and intercession. It is not that anything is wrong with these things, but they can clutter our lives and take time that we could devote to prayer.

We need around-the-clock houses of prayer raised up in local churches and on college campuses. Houses of prayer that do nothing but cry out to God for the forgotten areas around the world. The spiritual power it is going to take to see the gospel planted around the world and millions thrust into the Kingdom can only be sustained by these prayer furnaces. God knows that prayer and intercession must once again become our primary tools of moving forward appropriately and powerfully in global harvest.

Many Christian colleges or universities in the West have an annual "Missions Week" during which global prayer is offered at chapels. Most national campus ministry organizations have a "Missions Night" at their regional conferences. This is a small token of our thoughts and prayer given to God's global activity, while He's waiting for those who will lead the way and take up His banner for the "house of prayer for all nations" to be built up.

Let me challenge us to consider the many ways to increase fervent prayer for the forgotten in our own community of believers. Perhaps the Lord would have campuses initiate a day and night prayer room for global harvest and multitudes of message bearers to be raised up that spans the semester or academic year. This can happen if each person commits to a time slot of twenty minutes, a half hour, or an hour a couple of days a week. Maybe He is asking fellowships and campuses to host a monthly all-night prayer watch (11pm 'til 6am) with much emphasis placed on focused and informed intercession for the forgotten nations. Why not meet together with a group of committed prayer warriors to intercede every morning at 6am before the day begins? I know many campus fellowships and communities taking up these challenges as I write, and it is very exciting to watch them seek to implement ongoing intercession, specifically for global harvest. Let's creatively raise our sights, count the cost, and pay the price for the sake of Jesus' honor around the world.

It's Time for Extraordinary Prayer

It is not just ordinary prayer that must be offered in these days. It is time for extraordinary prayer to become commonplace. What does this mean? In countries in Africa, Asia, and Latin America, in particular, it is common to find believers who practice devotion in prayer that many westerners are not used to – all-night prayer watches and fasting for long periods while devoted to radical prayer.

When was the last time we focused our prayer solely on the works of God going on around the world and for global harvest? When our prayer groups targeted a people group where the gospel has never taken root and in which no or few national believers exist? Do we cry out to God with all our heart, mind, soul and strength to bring breakthrough in the hearts of people and to strip the veil from their eyes? Do the people really get into our hearts, and do we stand in the gap in love and compassion for these who are lost? Do our hearts break over their physical, social, and spiritual conditions? When were we last willing to sacrifice our time, our work, our family, our school, and our friends to stay earnestly in prayer for that lost people, or that land held in darkness? When were we last willing to forego our comfort, our meals, our little entertainments—even our cell phones—to spend uninterrupted time in a group pressing into the heart of God? It is time to truly count the cost. It is a time of sacrifice, which entails making a choice, then walking steadfastly in discipline to adhere to that choice.

When we're honest, we realize that most of our prayer for global harvest (if it exists at all) is passing and not very engaging to us. It is time for a dramatic shift. Often in today's spiritual climate we find our prayers limited to our direct surroundings. God is calling us to raise our sights and allow Him to distract us so that we can get the world into our hearts. Our charge is to stay the course, stay on target. It is God who changes hearts, and God who calls his people to prayer.

Not only is prayer the vehicle God uses to break things wide open spiritually, it also changes the one who stands in the gap as intercessor. For example, SVM2 (Student Volunteer Movement 2) hosts "Abandoned Devotion Gatherings" on campuses in cooperation and unity with various campus ministry fellowships. These five-hour gatherings of students include extended times of worship, uncompromising challenges concerning repentance, embracing sacrifice and to become or send message bearers, and radical prayer to see the love of Jesus spread globally in our lifetime. A student at a gathering at the University of California at Berkeley came having absolutely no passion to reach the forgotten, but a great passion for prayer and revival on campus. After hours of focusing his adoration on the person of Jesus, praying for needs and people around the world, and hearing the challenge that God is raising up a generation of message bearers, he became convinced that he was to be one of these. He signed the Message Bearer Creed and is currently adjusting his future plans with this new vision in mind. Times of prayer concentration, where one loses sight of the world and personal problems, and begins to view everything through the eyes of Christ, cannot fail to change the heart of the individual. It is a time to see the forgotten as God sees them— as His children, whom He designed from the beginning to be His own, and for whom He weeps and sorrows, looking for the time when they too shall get to hear the Good News, and know it is for them. You cannot glimpse God's heart in prayer and go away unchanged.

The Call of the Hour

To help rebuild the student mission movement among the emerging generation, SVM2 is seeking to awaken a united and sustained prayer movement fixated on the forgotten. This is happening through the formation of Global Prayer Teams and the widespread hosting of Abandoned Devotion Gatherings on campuses.

Global Prayer Teams (for adults 18-28 years old) form in college and career ministries in churches, on campuses, and even in the market-place. They form wherever someone catches a vision for launching out in serious, devoted, and pointed prayer for the forgotten and is committed to bringing others together to pray and intercede on a regular basis. Similar to the cell group growth model, these groups reproduce when they reach eight to ten people. To order the Global Prayer Teams Guide and sign your group onto the Global Prayer Team network, visit www.SVM2.net.

In unity, multitudes are asking God to use this generation to see the fulfillment of the Great Commission in our lifetime. A faith goal has been set to raise up 50,000 Global Prayer Teams on college cam-puses and in student ministries that are mobilized to pray, like never before, for global harvest and revival.

Abandoned Devotion Gatherings are being used of God to provide a catalytic boost of passion for revival and to reach the nations in collegiate communities. Order an Abandoned Devotion Gathering Facilitation Pack from www.SVM2.net. It includes all the materials necessary to host a five hour campus-wide interactive worship and prayer gathering on a campus or in a local church.

BUILDING BLOCK # 3 - SURRENDERED GOING

The medium that God uses today to communicate His message is the same as it has always been. Romans 10: 14 & 15 says, *"…And how shall they hear without a preacher. And how shall they preach unless they* *are sent."*The apostle Paul continues in this same verse saying, *"How beautiful are the feet of those who preach the Gospel of peace, who bring glad tidings of good things!"* God is glorified when we set out to be obedient and answer His call to make disciples in another culture.

SEVEN REASONS TO GO TO THE FORGOTTEN...

1. The Lamb Is Worthy

Jesus is the Lamb of God, who takes away the sin of the world (John 1:29). He was the sacrificial lamb provided by the Father because we were not able to save ourselves from the depths of our depravity, wickedness, and sin. Revelation 5:12 records the angels in the heavenly realm continually declaring with a loud voice, *"Worthy is the Lamb who was slain to receive power and riches and wisdom, and strength and honor and glory and blessing."*

Because of His almost inconceivable example of full surrender to the Father, Jesus is worthy of every human being's total adoration and love. He is the centerpiece of history, the One who was, and who is and who is to come; the King who now rules and reigns on the throne in power. Through the cross, Jesus earned the highest place of honor above every other honor possibly given. He is worthy of our best efforts, of our complete obedience, and of the worship of those who presently might be hostile toward Him. He is also worthy of our extravagant love for what He loves – those who are perishing around the world due to a lack of relevant knowledge of Jesus Christ.

2. The Spirit Is Moving

There is every reason to believe that we are living in the most exciting times in the history of the missionary movement. In Luke 10:24 Jesus tells his disciples that, *"Many prophets and kings have desired to see what you see, and have not seen it, and to hear what you hear, and have not heard it."* Though we know Jesus was referring to Himself and the coming of the Kingdom of God in their midst, could we not say the same thing in our day concerning what we are seeing take place in the world over? I believe many global message bearers of the past would have given anything to see the fruits of their labor which we are reaping today. What they cried out for, worked for, and died for is coming to pass.

The number of people daily being added to the body of Christ world-wide averages 174,000, with 3,500 new churches opening every week.[viii] There are many extraordinary reports of miracles taking place, resulting in people finding faith in Jesus Christ and churches being planted.

And yet what remains to be accomplished seems to be the most difficult work imaginable in areas most hardened and hostile toward the gospel. In Matthew 24:14 Jesus states that, *"This gospel of the kingdom will be preached in all the world as a witness to all nations, and then the end will come."* In terms of statistics, if the emerging generation can be wakened today toward its God-given responsibility, it is plausible that we could be the generation that welcomes our Savior back for the reward of His sacrifice. Someone once said, "The wisest thing you can do with your life is to find out what God is doing in your generation and throw yourself entirely into that work."

3. The Lost Are Dying

For men and women around the world who do not believe in the work on the cross of the Lord Jesus Christ for their personal salvation, there looms ahead a day of incredible catastrophe. They have no idea what horror awaits them on the day of their judgment before Christ. Every day, more then 66,000 people die in areas where the gospel has never taken root around the world.[ix] What would we do if these 66,000 who die every day were individuals trapped in a well or a cave somewhere in the West? We would have our top experts working around the clock to save these helpless ones and our media teams would all be covering the event. Why do we, in the Church, see those around the world who are presently on course for a Christ-less eternity any differently? Why do we fail to make the effort necessary to see these come into the Kingdom of God?

4. The Poor Are Suffering

Throughout the Bible we see the tenderness of God's heart toward the outcasts of society. The poor are a marginalized group who have always received, and still receive, this tenderness of the Father. He calls us as His people to be servants of those who have little or nothing. Statistics estimate that there are over 1.3 billion people who live in desperate poverty around the world today.[x] Another two billion are considered very poor. Most of us cannot imagine this type of poverty. It is easy to turn away from and ignore this great reality facing the global community, but we do so to the Church's peril.

We know that there are no easy answers to the problems of poverty throughout the world, but as believers in Jesus, we know that He is the Answer to every problem that we can possibly face...even poverty! This simply means we can trust Him, as we partner with Him in working among the poor, to bring forth healing and wholeness where there once was only desperation, hopelessness, and brokenness. The issue of poverty won't disappear, but when hearts start to change, peripheral changes begin to take place as well. I hope it is not seen as an over-simplification to say Jesus really is the only answer to all of life's questions, problems and issues. He can alleviate suffering and produce the necessary changes in people's lives and surroundings through His incredible love, peace, and comfort.

I believe God is calling multitudes to work among the poor. Where are those who will hear the call of Jesus to practically love the least of these (Matthew 25:45) around the world? Jesus' parable of the sheep and the goats is a fearful reminder of the call of God to a practical faith that demonstrates itself by feeding the hungry, clothing the naked, visiting the sick, and taking in the stranger (Matthew 25:35-36). We need modern-day Mother Teresas and Amy Carmichaels to rise, go and out of their deep love for Jesus, love those who can give no love in return.

5. The Church Is Commissioned

Some of us have heard and read the Great Commission passage of Matthew 28 many times in our lives. But have we allowed the incredible revelation of it to get into the crevices of our hearts, to let the Spirit of God grab hold of us through it? Or have we read it through the lens of a hundred excuses why this commission does not refer to us.

The stark reality is that the church has already been commissioned and called to go whether we realize and accept it or not. In fact, the Greek form of the word "go" in Matthew 28 clarifies that going out as His witness, according to Jesus, was assumed, not commanded. It actually reads, "As you are going..." Jesus assumed that His disciples would be going out with the gospel. The Bible, our authoritative manual, starting in Genesis 12:1-3 clearly lays out that it is the heartbeat of God to see that all peoples of the earth are blessed, initially through the seed of Abraham and now through the Church of Jesus Christ.

Imagine if this paradigm seeped into Bible-believing churches around the world. No longer would pastors preach that you need a specific call from God to go to the forgotten, but rather, that you need a specific call to stay and serve in your home community. Imagine if instead of insisting that only those who are gifted in evangelism should go, pastors taught that Christ expected all of us to be willing to go. It doesn't require a unique gifting to go and share the Good News, and to bring Hope where there has been none. No longer would the numbers of those preparing to be local pastors be so high, while the numbers of those preparing as cross-cultural message bearers remained low – those going to forgotten areas of the world would outnumber those becoming pastors.

6.If We Don't GO, We Die Ourselves

A common problem many churches and fellowships face is that of becoming totally inward focused with a preservation mentality – a form of slow, painful spiritual suicide. We are most comfortable in a place in which we are familiar and to which we are accustomed, so we can begin to slowly focus only on that which is directly in front of us, clutching it tighter as we fear that we are losing even this. We can begin to think that our local outreach and global responsibility are not integral parts of our fellowship, and we don't understand that the very way to get out of this cycle is to discern and pursue God's local and global purposes. Because involvement with reaching the world for Christ is so pivotal to the purpose of God, a lack of concern and practical involvement with it will inevitably bring spiritual death. This has happened and can happen again to individuals, campus ministries, churches and whole denominations.

7.The Father Is Waiting

God is incredibly patient with His people. If we think that we have reason to be impatient with others or ourselves, let us remind ourselves of His unending patience with us both individually and corporately.

God is and has been waiting for 2,000 years to come and retrieve His precious bride. It is out of a passionate love for each person around the world that He refrains from coming to claim His own. 2 Peter 3:9 says, *"The Lord is not slow in keeping His promise, as some understand slowness. He is patient with you, not wanting anyone to perish, but everyone to come to repentance."* God wants everyone to have a chance to choose to believe in His Son, to love Him with all of their hearts and to become a part of His beloved bride. He is waiting and pleading with His people. This is a great motivator for our urgent involvement in partnering with Him to bring these, for whom He is waiting, to His feet in adoration.

This awakening of believers from the emerging generation focused on His global purpose is long overdue. Jesus has waited for thousands of years to fully enjoy his Bride – a Bride complete (all nations), a Bride trained (praying and ruling), and a Bride focused (carrying the goals of His heart). We go about our lives, marry, and enjoy companionship. He still waits. And we only give him a token of our time and energy.

The Call of the Hour

SVM2 is working with many organizations and ministries towards seeing 100,000 new message bearers raised up from national sending churches around the world and sent to forgotten areas for long-term ministry. There is nothing magical about the number 100,000, rather, it is a faith goal to work toward across the emerging generation to increase focus, urgency, and cooperation.

A few years back, while reading the biography of the late Christian music artist Keith Green, I found myself stunned to read that he and Loren Cunningham made a commitment in 1982 to travel together and use Keith's concerts as a platform to mobilize 100,000 new workers for global ministry.[xi] A month after making this commitment, Keith was killed in a tragic plane crash. I was taken aback by what I read because just two weeks prior to reading this account, I sensed

God impress upon me to ask Him for 100,000 from the emerging generation today who will flood the unreached nations with the love of Jesus for long-term ministry. I remember telling God in response, "Father, this is my heart and life's cry. Raise these 100,000 up for your glory's sake around the globe!"

If we consider the large number of evangelical believers in the emerging generation (ages 18-30) around the world, 100,000 long term message bearers is a very small percentage to expect. If the emerging generation can be awakened to God's heart for the nations and answer His call to global, cross-cultural ministry, 100,000 new message bearers is a very attainable number and should be bypassed quickly.

These laborers being sent through multitudes of indigenous mission agencies and structures is exciting, but not the end goal! The goal is the millions of forgotten people whom these laborers will minister life to and who will be thrust into the Kingdom of God as a result of their life-on-life interaction. I am personally asking God to use these 100,000 to reap a harvest of at least 10 million souls in the most difficult regions of the world.

Let's pray the following prayer together on a regular basis:

> *"Oh Father...Lord of the Harvest, raise up 100,000 new message bearers who are zealous for your name, full of humility, and of the power of the Holy Spirit and, bring forth a mighty harvest of souls from the least-reached areas of the world for your glory."*

To join with multitudes of others who are stating their intentions to serve God among the forgotten when they graduate, visit www.SVM2.net and sign the Message Bearer Creed.

BUILDING BLOCK # 4 - IMPASSIONED MOBILIZING

While at a large global gathering of global mission leaders in Thailand, a friend from New Zealand and I discussed the topic of cross-cultural ministry mobilization with several major international mission leaders. We specifically asked them if they were aware of any training available for those who want to be equipped and prepared to effectively mobilize others for cross-cultural mission. They knew of no such training taking place globally. This astonished me as the reality facing the student mission world hit me: a lack of focus or adequate preparation for the biblical call of deliberately mobilizing the people of God unto His global purposes.

The Most Important Activity

Mobilizing others toward involvement in God's global purpose is one of the most exciting and strategic activities in which to be involved, especially as a college student. In fact, Ralph Winter of the U.S. Center for World Mission, has said that mission mobilization is the most strategic role in the missionary movement, and jokingly refers to those who "lost the vision and went to the field".[xii] Mission mobilization is rarely discussed or taught, and supposedly only done by those in "official" roles as mission mobilizers. This could not be farther from God's heart and it sucks the life out of the widespread student mission movement in our midst. All of us are capable of motivating and influencing our friends and peers on campus to catch their own vision of reaching the forgotten in our lifetime. All we need is a biblical understanding of God's heart for the nations, a passionate belief in the utmost importance of every person in every people group being given the opportunity to respond to the gospel, and a willingness and commitment to spread this understanding, awareness, and vision to every believer we might meet.

A Zealous Mobilizer

A little over fifty years ago, a Wheaton College student was convinced that to become a cross-cultural message bearer for Jesus was the highest and greatest calling a believer could have. He was still a student and couldn't go right then, so he set out to "convert" all of his friends and classmates to the central focus of going to the forgotten. He appealed to them to "throw aside their small ambitions" and commit to serve God overseas following graduation. He was quite radical and bold, offending some as he went about communicating the priority of global harvest. Through his influence, however, many message bearers chose to serve God globally rather than pursue careers in North America. His name was Jim Elliot. Taking his own advice, he mobilized four other men and their future wives to join him in Ecuador. During an attempt to contact the Auca Indians, a stone-age tribe in the jungles of Ecuador, all the men were speared to death. The tribe eventually came to Christ through the ongoing witness of the widows of some of the men. They are now reaching other tribes in the area. The story of these men and their martyrdom mobilized a generation of message bearers in the 50s and 60s. Thousands from that emerging generation dedicated their lives to serve God globally (my parents included). Jim Elliot's powerful story can be read in the book, *Through Gates of Splendor* by Elisabeth Elliot and has been made into a feature film entitled, *The End of the Spear*.

A Generation of Jim Elliots?

What if thousands of student leaders like Jim Elliot came to the forefront of our campuses and collegiate ministries? What if they each sought to engage, challenge and encourage their fellow students on campus or in their local churches with a vision of taking the gospel to the forgotten of the world? What if they pressed their peers for a commitment to go for at least two years, rejecting the postmodern mindset of not committing to anything in order to keep our options open? What if they promoted and catalyzed prayer for the forgotten on their campuses by organizing and coordinating global prayer teams? What if monthly large-scale gatherings were held to seek God for a prolonged length of time in worship and fervent global prayer?

I know what would happen! A generation would be wakened and activated with the mandate of going out in multitudes to touch a dying world with the love of Jesus Christ. It would become normal for students to become message bearers upon graduation. Many of them would be top students with incredible career prospects before them who choose to give these up in order to serve God among the forgotten. Presently we are seeing a few individuals on campuses here and there catch the vision and become involved in cross-cultural ministry following graduation. If this is all we want to see go into the global harvest then we can continue to do business as usual. But if we want to see the forgotten around the world worshipping Jesus in our lifetime, we need a new paradigm for mobilization. Historically, the most effective avenue for an awakening of this sort has been a grassroots student mission movement characterized by the four building blocks in this chapter (Extravagant Giving, Extraordinary Praying, Surrendered Going, Impassioned Mobilizing). It's time again to arise and diligently pursue the rebuilding of the student mission movement in order to waken the giant of the emerging generation.

Many students have a passion for influencing their campuses and ministries, but are not sure how to go about it. SVM2 has developed a complete training manual detailing how to proactively build a devoted student mission initiative on any campus or in a local church. This can be done within existing campus ministry fellowships on secular university campuses as well as on Christian colleges. Visit www.SVM2.net and order the Movement Manual. Throughout the process, helpful leaders are available to walk alongside the building, step by step.

As those whom God wants to use in this way, it is critical that we hold Jesus as the preeminent vision in our lives. God is seeking to cultivate in us a deeper and more mature consecration and devotion to Himself. Effective student mission movements of the past have been marked by those who were living first and foremost with abandoned devotion to Jesus Christ alone. Let's consider the central call of God upon our lives as we press in to lay hold of His fullness in our midst.

i   Ralph D. Winter, *Four Men, Three Eras* – Article
(Pasadena, CA: US Center For World Mission – William Carey Library) -
http://www.uscwm.org/mobilization_division/resources/web_articles_11-20-01/4_men_3_eras/4_men_3_eras.html

ii   Andrew Murray, *The Key To the Missionary Problem* (Fort Washington, PA: CLC Publications, 1979) p.97

iii   Ibid, p. 96

iv   Henrietta, C. Mears, *What The Bible Is All About* (Wheaton, Ill: Tyndale Publishers, 987) p. 575

v   Houston Perspectives Site - http://www.houstonperspectives.org/missionstrivia.html

vi   Pete Greig & Dave Roberts, *Red Moon Rising* (Lake Mary, FL; Relevant Books, 2003) p. 223 ff

vii   These seven are adapted with permission from a message Floyd McClung gave in July, 2003 - Unhindered Conference in Frisco, Colorado.

viii   Houston Perspectives Site - http://www.houstonperspectives.org/missionstrivia.html

ix   Bill Stearns, *Moving a Country* – Region by Region Article in Mission Frontiers, June July 1989

x   Ronald Sider, *Rich Christians* In an Age of Hunger (Dallas, TX: Word Publishing, 1997) p.1

xi   Melody Green, *No Compromise* (Eugene, Oregon: Harvest House, 2000) p. 263

xii   Ralph D Winter, *Is One Kind Of Mission Work More Important Than Another?* Article in Mission Frontiers – November-December 1991

"Yet indeed I count all things loss

for the excellence of the knowledge of Christ Jesus my Lord,

for whom I have suffered the loss of all things,

and count them as rubbish,

that I may gain Christ and be found in Him...

that I may know Him and the power of His resurrection,

and the fellowship of His sufferings,

being conformed to His death..."

PAUL IN PHILIPPIANS 3:7-10

"I HAVE BUT ONE PASSION - IT IS HE, IT IS HE ALONE. THE
WORLD IS THE FIELD AND THE FIELD IS THE WORLD; AND
HENCEFORTH THAT COUNTRY SHALL BE MY HOME WHERE I
CAN BE MOST USED IN WINNING SOULS FOR CHRIST."
Ludwig von Zinzendorf

CHAPTER 6

ABANDONED DEVOTION TO JESUS — THE KEY TO GLOBAL PROCLAMATION

In today's emerging generation, many are confused about the call of God. We may be living with busyness for God, but many of our lives are not marked by real fellowship with Jesus. We are not embracing this most important call. Do we really know Him?

God's highest call upon each of our lives is to get us into such deep and consistent fellowship with His Son that we become more and more like Him. God desires to form us into the image of Jesus even more than He desires to use us to accomplish His purposes.

In John 15:4-5, Jesus says to his disciples, *"Remain in me and I will remain in you. No branch can bear fruit by itself; it must remain in the vine… I am the Vine; you are the branches… Apart from me you can do nothing."* Can we claim to be His followers if we rarely take time to pursue Him wholeheartedly, to enjoy Him, and to commune with Him? Can we expect to impact a dying world apart from serious and consistent fellowship with Jesus, our Vine? It is imperative to our impact on the world that we know God experientially, and not simply talk about Him.

CALLED INTO FELLOWSHIP WITH THE SON

Paul, in 1 Corinthians 1:9 tells us that, *"God is faithful, by whom you were called into the fellowship of His Son, Jesus Christ our Lord."* The call of God is not to figure out what we're supposed to do with our lives, but to get into a vibrant and real relationship with the Lord Himself – so that when He speaks and begins to lead, we are absolutely aware of it. He longs for us to burn with desire to be in fellowship with Him, and to allow Him to birth His character and desires into our hearts and lives.

The Burning Heart of God

How do we do this practically? We must receive, by the revelation of the Holy Spirit, a real and deep understanding of the way God sees us. Once we see how He views us, we can choose to lavish love back upon Him. Why would we love someone we thought was always mad at us, or someone who we could never please no matter how hard we tried, or someone that wants to make us do something with our lives that we don't want to do? Many of us grossly misunderstand how God views us, and we are hindered from loving Him with a full heart.

We love because God first loved us. We love Jesus because we are deeply aware, not in our heads, but in our hearts, of the fiery passion with which He is consumed for each of us – those He created and for whom He died. He is turned upside down with joy and gladness when He thinks of us, which He does constantly! Since the foundation of the world, He has known us, been ravished with affection for us, and anticipated the day He could have deep and intense intimacy with us as we responded to His love. Our minds find this incomprehensible, which is why God must reveal it to our hearts and spirits.

A Progressive Revelation

It is only through this revelation that we attain any intimacy with Jesus. Further, this is a progressive revelation. He continues to unfold more and more to us as we show ourselves faithful with the portion that He has already shown us. As we seek Him diligently with all of our hearts, the Bible tells us "we will find Him" (Jeremiah 29:13). He wants us to consistently seek Him for more revelation, not being satisfied with how He revealed a portion of Himself to us last week, last month or last year. He wants us to continually know more of His heart. He knows that as our hearts become saturated with His view of us we will respond with fervent adoration back to Him.

A Personal Experience

When I was twenty years old the Lord began to open my eyes to these truths. For about six months, I experienced a tangible depth of closeness with Jesus beyond anything I'd known before or have known since. I found myself always wanting to be with Him. I'd skip my college classes, even declining to spend time with my friends, simply to have more time to fellowship with Him. He was making Himself and His heart toward me powerfully known. I would worship Him, study the Bible, and seek His face in prayer for hours and not get tired or bored. There was a hunger that burned within me to have more of Him. I could not get enough, and as I drew near to Him, He revealed His heart to me.

SITTING AT HIS FEET

He showed me that He desired all of His children to stay sitting at the feet of Jesus, seeking to understand how to abide in Him. Since then, when I've gone through wilderness times, feeling that Jesus was miles away, I have tried to continually bring myself back to Jesus' feet.

If we will abide in and worship Him in trying circumstances, or when we've been slandered, or when life just seems to be going down the drain, He will eventually lift us above the clouds of our situation to see through His eyes. Why? Because as we abide and worship, He softens our hearts to see Him for who He really is, which changes the way we see situations around us.

As we learn to sit at Jesus' feet, the following seven results of the abiding life (found in John 15:1-25) will begin to mark us. If these are not being cultivated more and more in our lives, we may need to reflect on how well we are fellowshipping with Him.

1) **FRUITFULNESS (JOHN15:5)** – This includes growth in character, maturity, functioning in our gifting, bearing the fruit of the Spirit, and impacting others through our lives.

2) **ANSWERED PRAYER (JOHN 15:7;16)** – As we abide in Jesus, our prayer lives change, and we begin to pray what's on His heart - for His desires, His will, His wishes, His purposes. The Bible promises us that when we pray His heart, He will respond.

3) **OBEDIENCE (JOHN 15:8-10)** – As Jesus makes our hearts more tender, we will want to please Him and obey Him. As we study the word diligently and with deep desire, we will see His ways more clearly, and know how to obediently walk in them.

4) **JOY (JOHN 15:11)** – Joy is different from happiness. Happiness comes and goes, but joy remains in us as we abide in Jesus, even when unhappy things surround us.

5) **SACRIFICIAL LOVE (JOHN 15:12-14;17)** – When we love other believers sacrificially, it signifies our ongoing intimacy with Jesus. His death for us showed us that true love is laying down

one's life for one's friends. When we give ourselves for others, Jesus makes sure we also are taken care of (Luke 6:38).

6) **HEARING FROM GOD (JOHN 15:15)** – Jesus confides in those with whom He has a close personal relationship. When we are abiding in Him, He can trust us with the secrets of His heart. His peace always accompanies His voice. There are many ways that God can and does speak. If we pursue Jesus rather than a formula, we will hear from Him.

7) **PERSECUTION (JOHN 15: 18-25)** – None of us likes persecution, but as believers, we can expect it. Persecution can be criticism with no apparent reason other than one's faith in God and commitment to follow Jesus. For those abiding in Him, this becomes normal.[i] It can also include actual bodily harm and martyrdom (Matthew 5:10).

All true ministry springs from each of our abiding relationships with Jesus. We can only give to others what we have first been given through being filled with His presence, His vision, His ways of doing things, and His very love. Are we willing to pursue God for those things with which He desires to lavish us?

A question I often ask myself is, "How much of God do I really want?" He is no respecter of persons. I can know Him as intimately as David, Moses, Abraham, Sarah, Paul, Timothy knew Him. I can have as close of a relationship with Him as John Wesley, Jonathan Edwards, Robert Wilder, Amy Carmichael did. The choice is mine, and it is a choice followed by determination, focus, and effort.

Do I persistently seek understanding and wisdom from the Lord, as Proverbs challenges me to (Proverbs 2)? Do I make it clear to Him that I desire to grow in Him consistently and obey Him wholeheartedly? Sometimes we look at great men and women of faith and envy their relationships with God. We covet the power in which they walked. Are we willing to pay the price that they paid to know God as they did? Are we willing to spend the sleepless nights, suffer the privations, give the time, and expend the energy that they spent to draw near to Him? Are we willing to answer His call to all-out faithfulness in a faithless generation? Are we willing to endure the heartache and personal pain that they did? Are we willing to be misunderstood by others (even Christians) in order to follow hard after Jesus? How much of God do we really want?

COSTLY ADORATION

The Lord is not impressed when we offer to Him that which comes easily and does not require much effort. In 2 Samuel 24:24-25 David shows us the importance of giving sacrificially to God. David is the king of Israel and the Lord tells him through the prophet Gad to erect an altar on the threshing floor that belongs to a common man named Araunah. David then goes to visit Araunah who sees him as he nears his land and goes out to greet him by bowing down before David and his servants. He asks why the King has come to visit his land. David responds by saying that he desires to buy Araunah's threshing floor on which to build the Lord an altar. Araunah then offers to give it to David as a gift, but David's response shows his correct understanding of the heartbeat of God. He says, *"No, but I will surely buy it from you. Nor will I offer burnt offerings to the Lord my God with that which costs me nothing."* We read in verse 25 that God heeded David's prayers for the land after his offering to God - something that cost Him something.

The deepest form of devotion or adoration is to give that which costs us something. This is true of any relationship. How far would we get if we gave our boyfriend, girlfriend, husband or wife only the kind of love that was easy for us to give? Most of them want all of our love, and so does God; in fact, He is jealous for it (Deuteronomy 4:24). He is pleased with those who, in response to His love, lavish back upon Him costly adoration and devotion. This communicates to Him our level of commitment and consecration. How can we offer to God today, out of hearts overflowing with gratefulness and thanksgiving, that which costs us something?

The woman in Matthew 26:6-13 gives us an example. While Jesus is at Simon the leper's house, a woman finds out that He is there and comes to Him with an alabaster jar of very costly fragrant oil. She then proceeds, seemingly without any introduction, to pour this costly oil on Jesus' head and anoint Him. His disciples criticize her for what they see as a waste of money that could have been given to the poor. Jesus, however, praises the woman for doing this, knowing it was her heart response of utter gratefulness and adoration unto Him. He then declares that this story of this unnamed woman will be forever recounted wherever the gospel is preached.

God records every act of true praise, devotion, and adoration that we offer to Him. He also knows our every failing and weakness, but in the midst of them, He sees our desire to please Him, even though at times we fail. In those moments following our repentance, He says, "I have forgotten your sin, rise up and move forward, allowing me to change you. I see your desire and commitment to love me, and it is wonderful to me." He knows our weaknesses, and even sympathizes with them (Hebrews 4:15), since He was tempted in the same ways that we are, yet was without sin.

The difference between true and false devotion lies in our motivation. Are we doing something out of habit or out of a deep desire to offer God all that He deserves, as the woman did? I often wonder how many of us, as we are told in our church services when to stand, sit, sing, and listen, are actually worshipping in a way that God receives and deeply enjoys. If we are motivated by anything other than a passionate desire for Him alone, God cannot bless it.

To have abandoned devotion to Jesus is to embrace the cross upon which He died, which seems to be quite costly. However, when our eyes are lifted up beyond our own understanding and we catch a glimpse of true Life, we realize that embracing the cross is not costly, but rather, a privilege and for our good. As we die more and more to self, we are formed more and more into the image of Jesus.

What does it mean to embrace the cross? Paul tells us that as believers, "...our old man was crucified with Him, that the body of sin might be done away with, that we should no longer be slaves of sin"(Romans 6:6). Through the cross, Jesus finished and accomplished the work of paying, once and for all, for the sin of all of humankind through His own shed blood. If we have believed this and trusted in His work as our only salvation, then Paul is saying that the cross also must be the place of our own death to self - our will, our ways, our pride, our irritability, our resentment, our critical spirit, our envy, and our worry – that we might be molded into the image of Christ. After this death, however, we join with Him in His triumphant resurrection and victory!

None of us can live the life of a true believer by "trying harder". Jesus wants to live His life through us. As we allow the self to be crucified on the cross with Jesus and as we yield all to Him, He is able to take control of our lives and live His own life through ours. If our self is still in control, He is not able to live through us. Admitting that we are dominated by self, then being willing to come to Jesus in repentance is the pivotal place of transformation.

Laying Down Our Rights

A major area of dying to self is that of laying down our rights for the sake of following Him and being useful in His hands.[ii] Jesus was the perfect example of One who laid down His rights for the sake of God and others.

He gave up first, and foremost, the right to be God. He left heaven to come to earth as a human being. He gave up the right of a normal birth and was born in a humble setting. He gave up the right to be with His earthly family. He left his mother to travel and minister. He gave up the right to marriage and to have a place to call home. He gave up the right to money. He gave up the right to a good reputation. In the end, He gave up the right to life itself.[iii]

One of Jesus' intentions in doing all of this was to show us how we are to live our lives. By laying down these things and losing them, Jesus was totally victorious. In the same way, we gain the whole world when we lay down our rights in every area of our lives (Matthew 10:39). Living our lives surrendered to Jesus, choosing to give up our rights to Him, identifying ourselves with Him, and allowing Him to be our all and all, is living with abandoned devotion.

We must choose to give these rights to Him. He will not force us to, but wants us to willingly say, "I love you and thank you for all you've done. I will follow you and lay down whatever 'right' that I hold near my heart because you are so incredibly worthy."

LOVE FOR JESUS AS THE MOTIVATOR
FOR GLOBAL OUTREACH

This may seem obvious, yet how many of us are compelled toward outreach by motives far below the standard of love for Jesus alone?

Maybe the fellowships in which we are involved tell us that we need to witness to others by going on a short-term mission trip. Maybe we want to look good as a follower of Jesus and promote ourselves. Maybe we are driven by religious guilt.

It is amazing how something as godly as reaching out to others with the love of Jesus Christ can become motivated by sinful intentions. If we're really honest with ourselves, we will see that our love for Jesus is mixed in with a host of other motivations.

I am grateful that God is patient, and that He disciplines us away from these lower motivations. He doesn't give up on us, but takes us through the process of getting rid of these things. I'm thankful that when we do reach out, even for the wrong reasons, He still uses us to minister to others.

God wants to mature us and bring us to a point where His love alone, overflowing from our hearts, is our motivation for outreach. He also wants us to realize that He doesn't judge us for our immaturity, but sees our heart's intention to reach out in love.

God doesn't want us to sit around until we think we are ready to love or serve purely, because we will never be ready. Instead, He wants us to reach out to others while we are allowing Him to make us new in our motivation. The processes are parallel.

GROWING IN ABANDONED DEVOTION

Many of us have only just begun our journey with God. We have received His love and are committed to starting well as His followers. We want to grow in prayer, faith, service and other disciplines. But we must also consider what it will take for us to live devoted to God over the long haul and to finish well. Many in the emerging generation do not consider this, and end up falling away from God after college or university.

A Disciplined Lifestyle

Discipline is the answer to producing faithfulness unto God throughout a lifetime. If we can learn the basics of the spiritually disciplined lifestyle now, we will have much to draw upon later in life. The discipline to which I am referring is learning to guard our moods, emotions, appetites, attitudes, thoughts, tongue, body, work ethic, and time. We also need to practice the spiritual disciplines[iv] of studying the Bible, praying, fasting, solitude, simplicity, meditation, serving others, and witnessing. To let God form and grow in us these areas of discipline is to have abandoned devotion to Jesus.

I suggest creating an action plan to remain disciplined in prayer, Bible study, fasting, giving, and witnessing to others. Many of us have great intentions to do these things, but the distractions of life easily keep us from these central disciplines. Why not take a three-month time period and write down specific goals for each category daily steps for fulfilling them?

Reinstating a Lost Practice

One of the lost spiritual practices of our day is that of reading. The stories of the history of the Church and of global mission are exciting and alive. Books can provide us with living examples of those who have been used of God before us, and we can partake of a powerful spiritual transference as we read the stories of old. Remember that Samuel Mills in 1806 was reading William Carey's words when his heart was penetrated with America's responsibility in foreign mission. He acted and history was made! Similarly Luther Wishard in 1877 was reading about Samuel Mills and how he and four others were used of God to birth the missionary movement in North America in 1806. He was instilled with a belief that his generation was responsible to finish what these had begun.

We have a rich spiritual heritage through which we can recognize the sequences of spiritual history, better understanding God's heart for our generation and our lives. By glimpsing in these books the spiritual principles that our predecessors lived by, and the way that God used them, we can adopt as our own their practices, prayers and dreams.

I suggest that we read a biography or Christian history book at least once every four months, letting the person's life motivate, convict, and teach us. Ask God to grow in us roots that go down deep into Him through the reading of others' lives. Some great biographies include Adoniram Judson, John Wesley, Amy Carmichael, Jim Elliot, C.T. Studd, Hudson Taylor, George Mueller, David Brainerd, Henry Martyn and J.O. Fraser. Condensed versions of these biographies can be found on the internet, and for a suggested reading list see Appendix A in the back of this book.

Hearing the Voice of God

Throughout this book I have regularly referred to the Lord as the One who speaks and communicates with us. As those seeking to grow in abandoned devotion, we must distinguish His voice from those things that are not His voice if we are to walk in faithfulness and fruitfulness in Him throughout life and in ministry. The Bible has countless passages that teach us about the voice of God. The real problem for many of us is that we have not cultivated what some have called the "hearing ear".[v] This hearing ear can distinguish the voice of God in the midst of the many competing voices in our daily lives (John10:27). Most of these competing voices fall into one of the following three categories: the voice of others (the world), our own imaginations (the flesh), or a thought that has been planted by the enemy (the devil).

Dick Eastman has been used of God all over the world to teach on the subject of prayer and hearing the voice of God. He suggests thirteen principles of divine guidance that are helpful for clearing up confusion regarding hearing the voice of God.[vi]

1) It is possible to hear God's voice (Colossians 1:9).

2) The purpose of all guidance is to know the Lord Jesus intimately (Philippians 3:20).

3) God speaks from where He dwells (Luke 17:21).

4) The Holy Spirit is heaven's representative in all true guidance (John 16:13).

5) God's word is the final judge in all guidance (2 Peter 1:19-20).

6) Guidance from God is always accompanied by the peace of God (Philippians 4: 6-7).

7) God speaks through various means (prayer, visions, dreams, visitations, voices, prophecy, circumstances, etc).

8) Most guidance from God comes unawares (Psalm 25:9).

9) Hearing God must prompt us to action (James 2:17).

10) Divine guidance comes from meeting God's demands (Isaiah 58:10-11).

11) Divine guidance does not mean that we will know the future (James 5:7-8).

12) Guidance is not always pleasant (James 1:2-4).

13) Guidance is a skill to be learned (Luke 11:1).

Eastman then teaches 6 dangers or errors in learning to hear the voice of God.

1) Assuming all guidance comes from God.

2) Thinking that God always uses spectacular means in guidance.

3) Basing all guidance on fleeces (Judges 6:36-40).

4) Valuing impressions, visions, and dreams above the word of God.

5) Misunderstanding circumstances in relation to guidance.

6) Ruling out the need for divine guidance.

The Bible teaches us to test the spirits (1 John 4:1-3). As those growing in our ability to hear God's voice, we must test the voices we hear. I learned a practice early in my walk with God. When I think I might have heard His voice, I take authority in Jesus' name over the voices of others, my imagination, and the enemy, silencing them and asking God to clarify whether or not it is Him who is speaking. With these other voices silenced through His authority, the thought, impression, or inner voice will either strengthen- confirming it being from Him, or disappear- proving it to be one of the competing voices.

This practice demands a discipline; listening and waiting. We cannot expect Him to speak if He knows that we are not actively listening. Would you speak to someone who wasn't showing you that they cared about listening to you? Will we put in the time and energy to wait and actively listen for His voice in the secret place?

Let me suggest six other principles that, if applied, will put us on the road to hearing from God on a regular basis.

1) **WE NEED TO WANT TO HEAR FROM GOD** – Without this desire, it is easy to mistakenly listen to that which is of the flesh, the world, and the enemy.

2) **WE NEED TO GET TO KNOW JESUS THROUGH READING AND STUDYING THE BIBLE** - We must discern if what we are hearing matches up to His word.

3) **CONSISTENTLY OBEY THE CLEAR TEACHING OF THE BIBLE** – Without obedience to His written word we become desensitized to His voice. Obeying what we already know of His guidance (the written word) will open up our hearts for specific guidance from the Spirit.

4) **LEARN TO MEDITATE ON THE WORD OF GOD** –This means to ask the Holy Spirit to show us specific meanings of Biblical passages for our lives. This entails growing in four areas: detecting the inner voice that God uses to speak to each of us, becoming still, seeing in the Spirit, and writing out dialogue with God.

5) **LEARN TO DISCERN THE SPIRIT** – The Spirit reveals specific truth to each of us. He reminds us of a certain Scripture in a time of need. He gives insight into certain Scripture for our lives. He gives insight into others' needs for ministry purposes. The voice of God will always complement the teaching of the Bible and the person of Jesus Christ.

6) **WE NEED TO STEP OUT IN FAITH WHEN WE ARE REASONABLY SURE THAT WE HAVE HEARD FROM GOD** – There will be times

when we are not absolutely sure what God is speaking to us. It is then that we should ask God for confirmation. We also need to realize, however, that He doesn't always give it. There is a degree of risk in hearing and responding to the voice of God. This is the life of faith that He is building into us.

In no way is this a exhaustive teaching on hearing the voice of God, but simply an attempt to give a few ideas to whet our appetites to the adventure of hearing His voice. I want to encourage us to seek the ability to hear His voice consistently. God will speak if we pursue Him with a pure and obedient heart.

EMBRACING THE SUPERNATURAL POWER OF GOD

Over one hundred years ago, Andrew Murray wrote the following in reference to the power that was released at Pentecost in Acts 2:

> *That Pentecostal generation did more to accomplish the evangelization of the world than any succeeding genera-tion. Considering the increase in the population of the world (in 1900) and the increase of the Church, we ought to do tenfold more than they did. But even if we are to do as much as they did, we need this one thing: to be filled with the Holy Spirit, as the power of God, to do the work of God! ...If there is to be any hope of our working like the Church of Pentecost, we must have a new era in our missions. There must be a real restoration of the Pentecostal life and power in the church at home. The power of God for the work of God must be the watchword for every worker.*[vii]

Building a life of abandoned devotion to Jesus and rooting ourselves in Him will inevitably bring us face to face with His call to live in the fullness of the Holy Spirit. Much of the body of Christ today embraces this fact, but this openness has been slow in coming. Many among the emerging generation recognize the importance of supernatural power in demonstrating and revealing the love of God. Lou Engle, leader of the Justice House of Prayer (JHOP) says, "Christian young people today are bored! Deep in their hearts they want to encounter the supernatural God of the Bible that does wild and unexplainable things."[viii]

Don't Throw the Baby Out

Due to abuses in the past, an understandable fear of the power of God marks many believers today. Yet we must not throw the baby out with the bathwater, and thus cut ourselves off from the very plan and purpose of God. Sometimes this fear comes because people have failed to show us a right and Biblical example of spiritual power, and other times it comes because we have been offended at a certain manifestation of power that we didn't like or understand.

As we consider reaching the world in our lifetime, we cannot leave out this most pivotal of Biblical truths. To do His work in His way and to ensure effectiveness and lasting fruit, we must embrace God as a supernatural God. He does things in a supernatural way and if we allow Him, will use us in this process to bring greater honor and glory to Himself.

The World Needs the Supernatural

Most of the world's forgotten populations have a worldview involving the supernatural. Humankind was created to have fellowship with God, who is Spirit. There is, therefore, a spiritual void within people that creates an ever-present spiritual hunger for the supernatural.[ix] As cultures around the world become more secular, the hunger in humanity for relationship with the supernatural increases.

But for too long many message bearers have gone out without an understanding of how to operate in supernatural power, or worse, haven't known how to combat the enemy when he shows up using counterfeit supernatural power. The enemy is more than happy to render us ineffective by keeping us blinded to our desperate need to walk in the supernatural power of Almighty God.

Paul tells us, *"For the Kingdom of God is not in word, but in power"* (1 Corinthians 4:20). It is important to have our doctrines organized, but Paul cautions that systematic theologies are not enough. Those who do not know the power of God place themselves and their ministries in tremendous danger. Satan has little trouble defeating these message bearers, because they do not know the Kingdom of God, which is characterized by power. Message bearers who believe the Word of God will be accompanied with power (Mark 16:17).

People need to see the power of God demonstrated in a host of creative ways in order for the gospel to take root. Part of contextualizing the message of the gospel to all men is bringing it to bear on the questions of the supernatural in their worldview. Paul writes *"I have become all things to all men that I might by all means save some"* (1 Corinthians 9:22). We must meet people where they are and show them, through power when necessary, that our God is the one and only living God.

Unexpected Power for His Glory

In Papua New Guinea, many years ago my dad had an encounter worth noting. While working on a portion of Scripture translation with an older man from the tribe who helped him understand the nuances of the tribal language, the man became sick with what the people considered a terminal illness. One day, my dad went to him while he was in bed asking for a bit of help with some difficult words. The verse he was stumped on was an account of Jesus healing someone. As they worked through this passage together, the man suddenly stopped, looked at my dad intently and asked, "Can this Jesus you've been talking about and that we are reading about really do this? Do you think He could heal me?"

This was a difficult situation for Dad. If he answered no, his faith would seem empty and without power. If he answered yes, and nothing happened, Jesus' reputation would be marred. He replied, "Yes, Jesus can heal you if He wants to!" The man immediately and enthusiastically responded, "Pray for me right now, that this Jesus would heal me!" Dad became extremely nervous as he imagined how the man would respond if nothing happened, but he put his hands on the man and asked Jesus to take away the sickness that was stealing the man's life. Nothing happened immediately.

After a few weeks, however, the man came to dad walking, something he had not done in a long time, and declared that he felt ninety percent better and had been healed. "I've been healed by Jesus! I've been healed by Jesus!" he declared emphatically. In a few more days he had fully recovered. He honored God and declared that he would from now on follow Jesus. Word of this supernatural healing spread through the village, and prepared the hearts of the villagers to follow this Healer, Jesus, as an indigenous church.

To go into the nations without embracing the supernatural power of God is to go in a way that God never intended. Paul writes *"I was with you in weakness, in fear and in much trembling. And my speech and my preaching were not with persuasive words of human wisdom but in demonstration of the Spirit and of power, that your faith should not be in the wisdom of men but in the power of God"*(1 Corinthians 2: 3-4).

Why does God work like this? Firstly, it is His supreme desire to receive all honor in every situation. If we, as His message bearers, can take credit for anything that has happened, He does not receive full honor. When the supernatural occurs it is harder for any person to take credit for it. Secondly, if people put their faith and trust in us, our words, our personalities, our programs, etc, they will be disappointed because we will fail them. But if they trust in the power of God, the foundation of their faith in Jesus is solid.

What About Me?

Jesus wants us to desire to partner with Him in seeing the Kingdom of God expanded through demonstrations of His power, but He will not force it on us. Ask Jesus for the filling of the Holy Spirit, who empowers us to minister in the supernatural gifts for the glory of God. Jesus said, *"…you will receive power when the Holy Spirit comes upon you; and you will be my witnesses…to the ends of the earth"*(Acts 1:8).

There are three general steps to receiving the Holy Spirit's power. First, we must surrender all known sin to Him and renounce it. Becoming full of the Spirit is about emptying ourselves so He has room to operate. We give control of our lives to Him with no strings attached. Second, we are called to obey Him. If we have truly surrendered ourselves to Him, we will seek to obey Him at all times. Third, we believe in His promise to fill us with His power. Faith is an integral piece here. Too often we don't "feel" something and so disregard the whole thing. After we've prayed expectantly to be filled with power, we can expect God to answer, and must give Him freedom to use us as He pleases, even in ways that we may not be used to or understand.[x]

i   Bobby Clinton, *Clinton's Biblical Leadership Commentary* (Pasadena, Ca: Barnabas Publishers, 1999) p. 312-314

ii Loren Cunningham, *Making Jesus Lord* (Seattle, WA: YWAM Publishing, 1988) p.18

iii Ibid, p.18

iv One of my favorites on spiritual disciplines is Richard Foster's *Celebration of Discipline* (San Francisco, Harper Collins, 1978)

v   Larry Lea, *The Hearing Ear* (Altamonte Springs, FL: Creation House, 1988) see chapters 2-3

vi Dick Eastman, *Challenge the World School of Prayer Manual* (Every Home For Christ, 1991) p.159-167

vii Andrew Murray, p. 89

viii Lou Engle, *Preaching Tape – Dreams*, Harvest Rock Church, March 10, 2002

ix Rick Joyner, *The Surpassing Greatness of His Power* (Charlotte, NC: Morning Star Publications, 1996) p. 140

x   There are many great books that teach about spiritual gifts and functioning in them. The ones I recommend include *Concerning Spiritual Gifts* by Donald Gee, *Developing Your Giftedness* by Bobby Clinton, and the *Gifts of the Holy Spirit* Series by Gordon Lindsay.

God be merciful to us and bless us,

and cause His face to shine upon us,

that Your way may be known on earth,

Your salvation among all nations.

Let the peoples praise You, O God;

Let all the peoples praise You.

Oh, let the nations be glad and sing for joy,

for You rule the peoples justly,

and govern the nations of the earth.

Let the peoples praise You, O God,

let all the peoples praise You.

Then the earth will yield its harvest;

God, our God, will bless us.

God will bless us,

and the ends of the earth will fear Him.

PSALM 67

THE PRIMARY WORK OF THE CHURCH IS TO
MAKE JESUS CHRIST KNOWN AND OBEYED AND LOVED
THROUGHOUT THE WORLD."

John R. Mott

CHAPTER 7

BARRIERS & ATTRIBUTES

The world has not yet been fully reached for the glory of Jesus Christ. Due to this, we must identify the barriers – especially the theological barriers – that are preventing the emerging generation from understanding and internalizing the call to serve cross-culturally, so that we can deal with these barriers in our ministries.

THREE THEOLOGICAL BARRIERS FACING THE EMERGING GENERATION

Research for this writing indicates that the following are the top three theological barriers to the emerging generation being activated into global mission today – (1) a lack of Biblical teaching on sacrifice, (2) the question of the sovereignty of God versus human responsibility, and (3) the problem of universalism and the reality of hell. Let's look at these barriers in more detail.

1. A Lack of Teaching on Sacrifice

The first issue relates to the lack of teaching on the scriptural foundation of denying self and what this practically means for the emerging generation. We've already touched on this a bit in other sections of this book. George Verwer, founder and former Director of Operation Mobilization, agrees that this foundation is essential. He comments, "If there is going to be a powerful missionary invasion in our day, there must be a return to the standard of Jesus Christ and of the New Testament...Many of Gods' people, I believe, have missed his perfect will. I am not convinced that it is the will of God for all these people groups to have no witness."[i]

Michael Brown, in his book, *Revolution!* highlights five idols in North America that hinder the Church from experiencing corporate and personal revival, and hinder us from wholehearted commitment to the global harvest: addiction to entertainment, obsession with sports, worldly fashion, fleshly indulgence, and secular academics. He writes in opposition to these, "Gratification is not our God! Money is not our master! Lust is not our Lord! The flesh is not our focus! Our allegiance is to one God and Him alone. All competing ideologies must be defeated and denounced."[ii] John Piper agrees, saying, "(God) has an inexhaustible enthusiasm for the supremacy of His name among the nations. Therefore let us bring our affections into line with His, and for the sake of His name, let us renounce the quest for worldly comforts, and join His global purpose."[iii]

2. The Sovereignty of God or Human Responsibility?

The tension between the sovereignty of God and the responsibility of His people in seeing the world reached for Christ has been in debate for hundreds of years and has staunch proponents on either side. However, the abuse of the teaching of God's sovereignty has caused many to think that personal involvement is not needed and that God will somehow draw people who have no way of hearing and internalizing the gospel truth to Himself on His own accord.

One of the verses used to defend this stance is Romans 8:29, which reads, *"For whom He foreknew, He also predestined to be conformed to the image of His Son, that He might be the firstborn among many brethren. Moreover whom He predestined, He also called…"*

Some understand this to mean that God is not only responsible for the entire process of salvation and sanctification, but has already predetermined who will respond to Him.

While it is true that God initiates the process by sending His Son and inviting us into relationship with Him, this argument neglects the fact that God has given us free will. Although God has foreknowledge and knows those that will believe in Him, He doesn't force people into relationship with Him. Ephesians 2:18 declares, *"For by grace you have been saved through faith…"*

It is only through what God has done and the way that He has provided through Christ (His grace) that we can be saved, but we lay hold of God's undeserved favor toward us through faith. Faith is born through our will, giving God the opportunity to speak to us through the Word of God. Faith comes by hearing and hearing by the Word of God (Romans 10:17). Though the Bible states in Romans 1&2 that no man is without excuse as creation itself speaks of a loving God, He chooses primarily to use us, sinful humans redeemed by His blood, to communicate His love to others.

3. Universalism and Hell

The final theological hindrance is universalism and the reality of hell. In our pluralistic, postmodern world, many in the body of Christ are quietly not sure what to make of hell. Though most Bible-believing churches assert that people will suffer eternally in hell apart from a saving relationship with Christ, some believers have a hard time bringing themselves to accept this truth deep in their hearts, especially in the face of a politically correct society that frowns upon any assertion of truth or discrimination of any kind. A campus ministry leader in Colorado said, "To adhere to something which cuts out such a large segment of society for such a horrible demise is seen as narrow and arrogant." It is a major problem specifically in today's secular student arena of North America. "Professors purposely seek out Christians in many of their classes to prove their spiritual beliefs wrong and to humiliate them publicly for believing in such ridiculous things," admitted a ministry leader in Indiana.

A mission leader added, "It is also quite difficult for some students to grapple with the fact that someone born in an Islamic country could be held accountable for something that their society utterly rejects. They are good people, would God really do that, they ask?" Those around the world who don't believe and are not in places where they can hear of Jesus and His love, prove the urgency of challenging the emerging generation to go to the places that lack a true Christian testimony.

Universalism is highly prevalent on most secular college campuses today, and will inevitably creep into the thinking patterns of believing young adults. The emerging generation needs to know why all religious belief does not, in the end, lead to God. It is critical that they think through their faith and become able to defend their convictions. Students want straight and real answers, not easy cliché responses.

Only Jesus Christ leads to the Father and ultimately, to heaven. A misunderstanding of this bedrock of Christian theology has gigantic implications for the global mission movement. Young adults reason that if those that live on the other side of the globe are not really lost and on their way to a Christ-less eternity, we don't need to go to them.

5 PRACTICAL BARRIERS FACING THE EMERGING GENERATION

We've talked a bit about the theological barriers that keep the emerging generation from becoming activated to fulfill the Great Commission. Now let's look at practical barriers that are holding the emerging generation from involvement: (1) parental influence, (2) problem of funds/faith, (3) the "American" dream, (4) they don't see themselves as message bearers, and (5) a sense of inadequacy.

1. Parental Influence

When those in the emerging generation tell their parents that they want to go on a summer cross-cultural trip, a large percentage are not supported and are actually told that they cannot be involved.[iv] Surprisingly, it is not only unbelieving parents who respond in this way, but also Christian parents. If this is the response when faced with a short-term summer trip, imagine if these students told their parents that they wanted to be long-term message bearers following graduation!

In Asian-American families, parents are especially resistant to the idea of their children becoming long-term message bearers. An Asian-American campus ministry leader in Boston noted, "Many Asian parents feel their children owe it to them to get a good job, since they sacrificed so much to bring them here to America." Thus many Asian-American students feel the pressure to please their parents before a desire to please and obey God.

Many students in Sub-Saharan African countries also face this dilemma. When one senses a call to long-term, cross-cultural ministry, there is a major tension with family because of a cultural expectation that children help support their family following graduation from university. A career as a cross-cultural message bearer will not provide the finances to do this effectively.

Another startling piece to this puzzle is that the emerging generation seems to desire the support and permission of their parents. A campus ministry leader in San Diego said, "They are more concerned today with respecting their parents." Possibly in the past, when a young adult was told by their parents not to go, he went anyways, for he was of age and on his own. It seems to be different now.

To see this barrier overcome, it is critical to teach the emerging generation how to put God first in their lives. Once they reach the age of accountability, they are responsible first to God and second to their parents and families. Yes, we seek to honor our mother and father according to the fifth commandment in Exodus (Exodus 20:12), but when their wishes come in direct contrast with the ways of God and how we sense the Holy Spirit leading us regarding our futures, we must remain strong and faithful to God first. For some this will be a test from God concerning where our ultimate allegiance is found. He may use it to force us to choose abandoned devotion unto Him.

2. The Problem of Finances

The perceived lack of funds is an age-old problem for cross-cultural workers. A leader in Indiana said, "Students today abhor the idea of raising support by asking others for money through letters, etc." Though many are discovering creative ways to raise funds for short-term trips, too many decide not to be involved even on short trips because they don't want to fundraise and it appears that there are no other options. This dilemma is multiplied a hundred fold for long-term workers. Some leaders among the emerging generation realize that it comes down to a fundamental lack of faith in God to provide the money. A campus ministry leader in Illinois remarked, "Most young adults today will not go the long haul, they'll have faith for a time and when something, even something small, stands in the way of that faith, they crumble."

I want to suggest that raising support and living by faith for finances is a wonderful blessing from God. My wife and I live by faith and the financial support of others. I say in all honesty that I absolutely treasure it for three reasons. First, it forces me to grow in faith and confidence in God, which I welcome. Second, it gives me the opportunity to build relationships with people who are not only giving, but also praying for me, building a necessary team to see fruit that remains. Third, I get to watch with anticipation as God moves in incredible ways to provide for my needs and the needs of those around me.

Jesus Himself lived on the support given to Him mostly by women. The Lord needed people to sow into His ministry and He needed to trust that God would provide this through whatever means He chose. His words of peace to us in Matthew 6:25-34 ought to be spoken over our fearful hearts as often as possible.

> *Therefore I tell you, do not worry about your life, what you will eat or drink; or about your body, what you will wear. Is not life more important than food, and the body more important than clothes? ... So do not worry, saying, 'What shall we eat?' or 'What shall we drink?' or 'What shall we wear?' For the pagans run after all these things, and your heavenly Father knows that you need them. But seek first his kingdom and his righteousness, and all these things will be given to you as well. Therefore do not worry about tomorrow, for tomorrow will worry about itself. Each day has enough trouble of its own.*

Student debt is another financial deterrent in the student world. With college expenses continuing to rise, more students are being forced to take out hefty loans, which are a significant problem to financial freedom later.

One way to overcome the financial barrier is to combat the idol of materialism in our midst. A second way is to learn how to trust God for our finances, seeing this as a realistic and biblical form of living. A third way is to challenge the lure of credit cards. Some loans for school are necessary, but we can control other forms of accruing debt. We need to display self-control and keep our debt to an absolute minimum in order to be free financially as soon as possible, allowing us to get overseas quickly.

3. The False Idol of the "American Dream"

The subtle, creeping temptation to pursue the "American Dream" has robbed the missionary movement of many competent and gifted laborers. The "American Dream" for the current generation isn't necessarily a house and white picket fence, but more of a lifestyle free of restrictions, even that of a job. These want time to be involved in the activities about which they are passionate.

We all want to follow society's choreographed way for "making" it. Yet Jesus' measure of success is completely different, as Loren Cunningham says: "If you try to save your life, you'll lose it. But if you lose it for the Lord's sake and the gospel's, you'll save it. Jesus did it. He humbled himself as far down as anyone could possibly lower themselves. That same Jesus is telling us to follow Him. Take up His cross. Become a slave. Lose your rights and you'll win the kingdom." [v]

4. "I'm Not a Missionary"

Many in the emerging generation simply do not see themselves as a "missionary" in the traditional sense, and thus do not even consider getting involved. Robertson McQuilkin, in his book The Great Omission lists five reasons why global mission suffers – (1) we don't care that much, (2) we don't see very well, (3) we think there must be some other way, (4) our prayer is peripheral, and (5) someone isn't listening.

Expounding on this list, Roger Greenway notes:

> *Missions suffers because lukewarm Christians don't much care about the things that Christ cares about supremely. Missions suffers when Christians are ignorant of the needs of the world and don't see the billions who are unsaved, unchurched and uncared for. Missions suffers when church members assume that if God wants the unevangelized peoples of the world brought to Him, He'll do it somehow. They sense no need to pray about it or get personally involved in it. Missions suffers when the subject is not preached and taught from Scripture, and the Church doesn't hear the heart throbbing call to go forth and evangelize all nations and peoples.*"[vi]

The emerging generation has evidently not been adequately taught about the call and the spiritual gifts God has unleashed upon us to fulfill that call. Some may simply look at themselves and assume they are not a public speaker and take themselves out of the running for cross-cultural ministry. They eliminate the possibility of seeing themselves as a message bearer of any sort. Yet each of the spiritual gifts is necessary to properly advance the gospel, not just those of evangelist and pastor. There are no favorite gifts in God's eyes, but all are critical to the speedy completion of the Great Commission. The old stereotype of a "missionary" has changed drastically. (See chapter 9 for more information concerning what a message bearer in this generation might look like.)

5. Sense of Inadequacy

A few years ago I spoke at a student mission conference in Chicago. Just prior to my session, the group of intercessors who had been praying in a back room throughout the conference approached me saying they sensed that many of the young adults in the audience were feeling bogged down with guilt because of prior sin in their lives. The intercessors felt this guilt was leading them to feel inadequate and unable to respond to the challenge of involvement in the global things of God that they were hearing about. Hearing this, I changed my message slightly, focusing on the call to freely receive the grace of God and to forgive ourselves of past failings. Many students responded and were set free that afternoon from areas of bondage.

Over the last few years I have come to believe that this barrier – feeling inadequate because of failure and sin – is Satan's primary tactic for keeping believers in the emerging generation from reaching their full potential and destiny in God. Because of the sin-riddled society in which we live, many of us have come out of lives that were worldly and immoral. This is why we are so grateful to Jesus for His mercy and compassion, "...*in that while we were still sinners, Christ died for us*" (Romans 5:8).

The problem comes when we receive the forgiveness of sin through Jesus' blood, are born again, but then cannot seem to forgive ourselves for things that we have done. Psalm 103:12 is a revolutionary verse to those who take it to heart. The Psalmist declares, "*As far as the east is from the west, so far has He removed our transgressions from us.*"

And the prophet Isaiah declares under similar inspiration of the Holy Spirit, *"I, even I, am He who blots out your transgressions for my own sake, and remembers your sins no more."*

When Satan plants lies in our minds about our past sin and tells us that we are not adequate to serve God, we can tell him very matter-of-factly that every sin committed in our past is under the blood of Jesus and that He remembers them no more. This is the Sword of the Spirit that cuts the enemy down. He is a liar, a deceiver and only distorts truth. He wants to bind us up with wrong ways of thinking about ourselves, and more importantly, wrong ways of thinking about God. We may remember our sin, but God doesn't. He has no recollection of it when we confess and repent.

A very real truth that needs to be restored to the emerging generation is that God gives all-powerful grace to overcome and walk in victory throughout life. This grace is an unending and limitless resource to us. As Jesus told Paul, *"My grace is sufficient for you"* (2 Corinthians 12:9). His point was that Paul could consistently draw upon a tangible strength and power that Jesus is ever ready to give to those who come to Him. The grace (power) to walk victoriously is there; we simply have to take hold of it and receive it in our situations by faith. The grace (power) to know that we are truly forgiven and washed in the blood of Jesus is available. Our responsibility is to simply receive it in the midst of difficulty and temptation.

God's forgiveness sets us free from bondage to our prior sin, and His grace empowers us to continue in freedom. None of us can claim any strength of our own when we stay free of sin – it is because of His grace along. Let us receive His grace today and not allow the enemy to keep us bound and useless in the hands of Almighty God.

The apostle Paul is our example. He says about himself, *"Christ Jesus came into the world to save sinners, of whom I am chief"* (1 Timothy 1:15). If the apostle Paul, the same one who persecuted and killed many Christians, became the greatest message bearer ever after coming into contact with the risen Savior (Acts 9:1-9), there is hope for each of us! We must forgive ourselves, receive His grace, and move on toward God's purpose in our lives. In ourselves, we are hopelessly inadequate, but because of Jesus, we are deemed adequate!

ATTRIBUTES OF THE EMERGING GENERATION

Many Christian leaders today believe that God is going to do some amazing things through today's emerging generation. They frequently use terms like "the revival generation" and "the generation of destiny". What attributes of this generation support such a belief? Obviously, they are diverse and unique individuals but it is possible to discern attributes that characterize the whole generation.

Let us examine, in no particular order, three positive and three negative attributes that characterize the potential for the involvement of young adults in the global harvest. Positively, the emerging generation is (1) culturally sensitive (2) community focused, and (3) desires meaning in life. Negatively, we find (1) pluralism and a fear of imposing oneself, (2) materialism and a consumer mentality, and (3) an inconsistency in character.

POSITIVE ATTRIBUTES

1. Culturally Sensitive

Research conveys that young adults today are well aware of the differences between people, and are more likely to embrace and love those who are different.[vii] Because many are well-traveled, they have met different kinds of people who think all sorts of wild and different things. "These guys are more cross-cultural in their thinking and in their actions than any previous generation in history," concluded a mission leader in Wisconsin. They exhibit a genuine desire to learn about others and to sympathize with their hardships and experiences (evidenced in the growing interest in social justice and development work). This is an attitude that well equips them to be message bearers.

2. Community Focused

Community is everything for the emerging generation.[viii] A campus pastor at a Christian college in Indiana remarked, "Their loyalties to one another are very strong." Another campus ministry leader in Colorado challenged, "Unless we have a massive overhaul in the way we recruit message bearers, we will miss this generation. They don't care where they go as long as they have a strong team to go with. The question used to be, 'where is God calling me to go?' Now the question asked is 'who is God calling me to go with?' If they have a community where depth of relationship is strong, conflict is worked out and not ignored, they'll go to the hardest places in the world." This value placed on community has incredible evangelistic possibilities as most cultures in forgotten areas of the world value community and depth of relationships very highly as well. Many people have come to faith in Christ through observing the loving interaction of a team of message bearers in community.

3. Desires Meaning in Life

God has created humankind to long for meaning. When people are awakened to who they are in Christ, they desire to live lives that matter to God. A campus leader in Kansas said, "The emerging generation possesses an overwhelming desire to matter and to make a great impact upon their world."

Something to watch out for here is hype. A common mission challenge to young adults has been to "do something significant" without giving them adequate teaching or training on what it means to "do something significant". A student in Texas voiced this concern saying, "There is an inherent problem in this because our generation is very feelings and emotions based. When we get to a country and get into the mundane things of our work and come up against problems and walls, etc. we don't feel very significant. So we feel ripped off or lied to. We read the books of the great missionaries of the past and romanticize what being a message bearer is all about, instead of understanding that it is important and significant, yes, but hard and lonely and tiresome all the same!"

NEGATIVE ATTRIBUTES

1. Pluralism and Fear of Imposing Our Faith

This is the other side of being culturally sensitive. A desire to be sensitive to cultural differences in people can lead to a dangerous pluralistic and relativistic outlook. We may water down what we know to be truth and seek to accommodate other people's beliefs and thoughts, giving the impression that we don't fully believe what we say. Right tolerance is to love people no matter what they believe, but not to accept their belief as equal to our own.

Because of negative postmodern influences, it is easy to adopt the prevailing mindset that each person chooses the beliefs that suit him or her the most, and all are equally valid. "Pluralism is a huge problem on college campuses these days. No one wants to step on other people's toes," related a campus ministry leader in California. Another leader in Texas reasoned, "The worst thing for a student to be called today is narrow-minded and this will be the lot of a Christian who is vocal about their faith on campus."

2. Materialism and the Consumer Mentality

A.W. Tozer writes, "Christianity will always reproduce itself after its kind…not the naked word only but the character of the witness determines the quality of the convert… The popular notion that the first obligation of the Church is to spread the gospel to the uttermost parts of the earth is false. Her first obligation is to be spiritually worthy to spread it!" "[ix]

God has called us to seek first His Kingdom. Many believers, however, primarily in the North American setting, are more fixated on the latest styles, cars, and bands than upon the things of God. An inflated materialism in our hearts should be the first sign that something is not right. God has called us to live simple lives without getting caught up in the love of things as the rich young ruler did (Luke 18:18-23). Do the things in our lives own us, or do we own them? If God asked us to give them away, could we? There is nothing wrong with having things. There is a lot wrong, however, with them holding us back from faithfully following God in obedience and faithfulness.

3. Character Issues: A Generation Killer

The character of younger believers is a major crisis today. "A basic problem with these young people is that they are inconsistent in character," conveyed a mission leader in Texas. Today's young adults face more blatant temptations than any previous generation.

There are a multitude of areas that need to be openly discussed. One particularly powerful area of sin in our day is the use of internet pornography. Some leaders believe the reason behind the lack of male spiritual leadership rising among the emerging generation is shame and guilt over their use of pornography. A campus leader in California said with tears in his eyes, "We're losing a whole generation of male leaders to this thing. They won't step up because they feel unworthy, yet they love God dearly." Another leader in Texas remarked, "My organization did a study and found that the two primary reasons behind why a person is rejected for a staff position with us are homosexual tendencies and internet pornography."

Previous studies have shown that the emerging generation is the most Biblically illiterate generation yet. Could there be a parallel here? It would seem that the call of the hour is to greater discipline and discipleship. Spiritual disciplines equip young believers with the tools to live in victory over sin through the power of the cross. It is not an overnight process but one that young adults must choose day by day. The emerging generation may have all the passion in the world, yet need desperately to heed the words of Moses to the Israelites as God's words for us today, *"Fix these words of mine in your hearts and minds; tie them as symbols on your hands and bind them on your foreheads* (Deuteronomy 11:18)." It is by reading, studying, meditating on, and obeying the Bible as consistently as possible that we learn and grow in the deeper ways of God and are encouraged and strengthened to turn away from our sinful and flesh-driven ways and embrace His better way; the abundant life in the Spirit (Galatians 5: 16-26).

In the next chapter, we will transition from looking intently at the emerging generation to observe the key attributes of the movement itself.

i   George Verwer, Address at The World Consultation on Frontier Missions, Edinburgh, 1980, Article in Seeds Of Promise, Allan Starling, ed. (Pasadena, CA: William Carey Publishers, 1981) p.184

ii   Michael Brown, Revolution! The Call To Holy War (Ventura, CA: Regal Books, 2000) p. 148

iii   John Piper, p. 40

iv   Ryan Shaw, p.44

v   Loren Cunningham, p. 145

vi   Roger Greenway, John Kyle & Donald McGavran, Missions Now: This Generation (Grand Rapids, MI: Baker Book House, 1990) p. 35

vii   Ryan Shaw, p.39

viii   Ibid, p.39

ix   A.W. Tozer, Of God And Men (Harrisburg, PA: Christian Publications Inc., 1960) p. 37

After this I looked and there before me

was a great multitude that no one could count,

from every nation, tribe, people and language,

standing before the throne and in front of the Lamb.

They were wearing white robes

and were holding palm branches in their hands,

and crying out with a loud voice, saying,

"Salvation belongs to our God

who sits on the throne, and to the Lamb!"

REVELATION 7:9-10

"I HAVE FOUND THAT THERE ARE THREE STAGES IN
EVERY WORK OF GOD; FIRST IT IS IMPOSSIBLE,
THEN IT IS DIFFICULT, THEN IT IS DONE!"

Hudson Taylor

CHAPTER 8

CHARACTERISTICS OF THE INTERNATIONAL MOVEMENT

What does an international, widespread, and history-making student mission movement look like today? Let's take a step back from our immediate campus or local church communities to view the big picture. An individual is personally awakened to their global responsibility, and soon they are influencing others on their campus through a campus mission initiative. The fervency of this initiative flows into the local churches in the area and eventually to other campuses in the region. If enough areas and regions are activated, and if they communicate with each other, and agree upon common points of prayer and goals for their region, a sense of united momentum emerges. This is the potential national student mission movement across a given country. As ministries and organizations serving the emerging generation around the world begin to implement similar strategies and points of focus, a massive and widespread international movement occurs.

Certainly this movement shares some of the characteristics of other historic movements (see chapter 3), but these characteristics take on modern personality and this movement includes facets not seen in previous movements.

One of the emerging trends we are seeing in international ministry circles is that of networks and collaborations. God seems to be highlighting His desire for His body to function in unity in order to lay hold of His purposes instead of continuing to do things as individual organizations, churches, denominations, and streams. We can do more for the kingdom when we come together under a common vision and banner and work towards a broad goal using our combined resources and efforts. With technology increasingly connecting our world, this becomes all the more possible.

WHAT IS A MOVEMENT?

Bobby Clinton of Fuller Seminary has studied historical, Biblical, and secular movements for many years, and has found that every movement is characterized by five common commitments of its participants, which must also characterize our student mission movement today. He defines a movement as a "groundswell of people committed to a person or ideals and characterized by the following important commitments":[i] (1) Commitment to personal involvement, (2) Commitment to persuade others to join, (3) Commitment to the beliefs and ideals of the movement, (4) Commitment to participate in a flexible, non-bureaucratic cell-group organization, (5) Commitment to endure opposition and misunderstanding.

EIGHT CHARACTERISTICS

The following are eight characteristics that leaders among the emerging generation describe as the critical features for rebuilding the student mission movement today.[ii] Some of the subjects are considered in more detail in other portions of this writing.

1. Deep & Consistent Prayer & Revival

The student mission movement can only be revitalized insofar as the lives of those involved in the movement are renewed. We must more intently fix our eyes upon Jesus. I have found that many who are pursuing revival in their communities are viewing it as an end in itself. We should not be seeking revival to for revival's sake, but rather, wholeheartedly seeking Jesus. If He is exalted as the pre-eminent One in our midst, the deep spirituality that leads to true revival will be hastened and the mission movement that accompanies it will spring forth.

Though many in the Church are still not awakened to the reality that life is a war, pockets of those that do understand dot the landscape of the world. They are the ones who are shaping global history. Walter Wink said, "History belongs to the intercessors." John Piper writes, "Life is war. That's not all it is. But it is always that. Our weakness in prayer is largely owing to our neglect of this truth. Prayer is primarily a wartime walkie-talkie for the mission of the Church as it advances against the powers of darkness and unbelief."[iii]

The success of any advance of the gospel parallels the tenacity of the intercessors involved in the effort. So what kind of prayer is needed for the student mission movement today? Spirit led, prophetic, warfare prayer for the forgotten, yes, but also for the college campuses in various parts of the world where Christians are found, in order that God might sweep through campuses igniting and aligning hearts with His own for the forgotten.

2. Cross Denominational/Inclusive

The second characteristic of unity among denominations, organizations, and ministries is not only attainable but already taking place right before our eyes. Leader after leader voices the desire to partner with others in better equipping the emerging generation. The realization that they don't have to lead alone is spreading like wildfire. Although there almost inevitably remains competitiveness, jealousy, and envy, the body of Christ in the student world as a whole is recognizing their need for oneness. It is imperative that we repent for allowing pride to tell us that, "We have it all and don't need each other."

Until recently, a united mission vision and goal among the emerging generation has been non-existent. The body of Christ as a whole has had various unifying mission visions over the years, such as the Lausanne Committee for World Evangelization, the former AD2000 and Beyond Movement, and the World Evangelical Fellowship Missions Commission. But the emerging generation has generally been without one. It is vital that today's student mission movement reach across lines of affiliation and, call students, above anything else, to a lifetime of personal involvement in God's global purposes. As revival historian David Smithers says, "Missions is not another option, but something that demands a response!"[iv]

The first measurable response to this call is to commit to going for at least two years (a call used in North America as other national student mission movements internationally develop a time commitment that is applicable to their contexts). There are many mission organizations with a sufficient structure available to send multitudes of message bearers for an initial term of two years (and longer). Most campus ministry organizations have mission arms that can easily place students in a wide variety of mission work, preferably in areas where the forgotten live. Yet we know there are also new structures and organizations that need to be created to effectively see the emerging generation trained and strategically sent out to see the Great Commission completed in our lifetime.

3. A Big Vision of God

As the contagious movement is being built, we must ask God to expand our revelation of His greatness. Is our view of Him too small? We need to assess our own views of God and what motivates us with what Floyd McClung calls "Apostolic Passion". He states that, "If you live without a vision of the glory of God filling the whole earth, you are in danger of serving your own dreams of greatness, as you wait to do 'the next thing' that God tells you. There are too many over fed, under-motivated Christians hiding behind the excuse that God has not spoken to them."

The student mission movement is characterized by renewed faith and utter trust in the unchanging Word of God. Those involved take God at His Word and trust Him to fulfill His promises to them and through them. As they go forth in obedience they hear Him speaking, "I am with you and I have overcome the world." They also are the ones who hold high the standard of the Scriptures and refuse to let common sense, pluralism or relativism skew the Scriptures for them. '

4. A Renewed Lordship Encounter

Only those who walk with Jesus as Lord will be able to plant the gospel in the least-reached areas of the world. Is He really in control? Is He really empowering us? Can we confidently rely on Him in the midst of hardships, discouragements, setbacks, etc? We need an army of young people who are like the martyr Stephen, who was *full of faith and of the Holy Spirit* (Acts 6:5)." Such message bearers will not back down when the going gets tough, as it most certainly will.

5. Campus Fellowships Devoted To Mission

A mission leader asked, "What if groups were set up on campuses that were entirely devoted to missions?" Could this work? Other leaders agree that such groups are vital to seeing a vibrant and influential student mission movement, creating an environment of prayer and intercession that is a precursor for any revival. Such growth in mission awareness, understanding, and the needs in the world, will foster in students a desire to go to the ends of the earth for long-term work after graduation.

When a fellowship or church takes its mission responsibility seriously, God blesses that group or church mightily with His presence and power. If we prefer those on the other side of the world, the Lord makes sure we are taken care too! The way to see revival in a given nation is to first become wholeheartedly committed to reaching the forgotten around the world.

During the Student Volunteer Movement, groups of students called "bands" formed on campuses throughout North America. They were from various campus ministry organizations that existed at that time and they remained a part of them. Yet they gathered together as groups within their fellowships around the common vision of raising up student vision for reaching the world in their generation. The Bands did not compete with campus ministry organizations. Instead within each of them they developed focused groups committed to the nations which were networked nationally. They were zealous and steeped in prayer. And it was nothing less than the Spirit of God that was infusing this vision into their hearts and minds. God will do the same today as students create student mission prayer teams and fellowships in order to see the Great Commission fulfilled in our life-time within campus ministry organizations like InterVarsity, Campus Crusade for Christ, Baptist Campus Ministries, and so on.

6. Creative Forms of Mission

There are incredible opportunities for creative and personalized ways of doing mission (see chapter 9). The landscape of how to do mission globally is increasingly changing. Many traditional laborers will not find access into the most desperately spiritually needy nations. The emerging generation needs to hear the message today that there is a place for each one in cross-cultural ministry according to what they are good at, what they love, and what they are professionally trained in.

7. Mentoring Between Older Generation Message Bearers and Current Message Bearers

Mentoring is necessary for every Christian seeking to live for God and wanting to be used by Him. Apart from these vital relationships we cannot succeed in what God has ordained for us. It is through this natural relational process that experience and values are passed on from generation to generation. The "self-made" man or woman is a myth.

Few try to walk through the paths of life alone, yet it is difficult to find people with whom to walk. Many organizations are seeking ways to implement innovative ways to foster mentoring. One organization is linking veteran message bearers who are now back in North America with students who are interested in missions.

This kind of plan could be implemented exponentially to bring forth a mountain of spiritual fruit. Because this generation highly values community and relationships, it seems more essential than ever to establish solid mentoring networks. A student will rarely make the decision to become a message bearer without the committed and consistent input of a few trusted individuals.

8. A New Apologetic for Global Mission

How can mission vision penetrate the hearts and minds of students today? When recruiting for global mission one hundred years ago, a person could simply speak of the needs abroad and the fact that millions were dying without Jesus, and it would be enough to bring forth the conviction of the Holy Spirit and thousands of commitments to be long-term message bearers.

During the '40s and '50s recruiters challenged students to help build up war-torn areas and practically serve the world. Today these same tactics don't work. One leader in Boston remarked, "Pictures of drunk people on the streets with songs like 'People need the Lord' playing in the background just don't do it anymore." A leader in Wisconsin agreed, "Students are asking harder questions about motivation today. The old clichés don't work."

In his book, *Let the Nations Be Glad*, John Piper has done the church a great service by giving us a new apologetic for mission. He focuses on the truth that mission is not really about the lost dying without Jesus. He brings us back to the reality that God is seeking to be glorified through the worldwide worship of Himself. When people are reached with the love of Jesus Christ, they turn from sin and receive forgiveness and mercy, bringing honor to God. He is passionately concerned with receiving this glory from all corners of the earth.

It is for the sake of His Name that we do global mission. Piper says, "All of history is moving towards one great goal, the white-hot worship of God and His son among all the peoples of the earth. Mission is not that goal. It is the means. And for that reason it is the second greatest activity in the world."[vi] This cry for the global honor, worship, and praise of God through every tribe, tongue and nation is our motivation, and it is upon this foundation that we build the student mission movement today.

i   Robert J Clinton, *Clinton's Biblical Leadership Commentary* (Pasadena, CA· Fuller Publishing, 1999) p.535

ii   Ryan Shaw, p.48-56

iii   John Piper, p.41

iv   David Smithers, Preaching Tape – *"Revelation and Revival"* (Teen Mania Missions Conference, 2001)

v   Floyd McClung, *Apostolic Passion*, Article in Perspectives On The World Christian Movement Manual (Pasadena, CA: William Carey Publishers, 1999) p.187

vii   John Piper, p.15

He shall have dominion also from sea to sea,

and from the River to the ends of the earth.

Yes, all kings shall fall down before Him;

All nations shall serve Him.

His name shall endure forever;

His name shall continue as long as the sun ....

All nations shall call Him blessed.

And let the whole earth be filled with His glory.

PSALM 72: 8,11,17,19

"HIS AUTHORITY ON EARTH ALLOWS US TO DARE TO GO
TO ALL THE NATIONS. HIS AUTHORITY IN HEAVEN GIVES
US OUR ONLY HOPE OF SUCCESS. AND HIS PRESENCE
WITH US LEAVES US NO OTHER CHOICE."

John Stott

CHAPTER 9

THE GLOBAL CHURCH ACTIVATED... GOD'S VEHICLE

More than ever, the whole Church around the world is embracing her God-given responsibility of making disciples among all nations! The western Church, which has historically played a larger role in sending message bearers to the forgotten, is now being eclipsed by non-western national churches. South Korea currently has the distinction of sending the most long-term message bearers per capita.[i] Nigeria recently launched its Vision 50:15, a campaign to mobilize 50,000 Nigerians over the next fifteen years to take the gospel through the North African Islamic nations back to Jerusalem.[ii] The southern portion of India is gaining ground as the Church raises up multitudes of her own to reach forgotten people groups throughout Muslim northern India, Pakistan and Bangladesh. Many in the Filipino Church believe they have all they need to be a major player in reaching Asia, as the Filipino Diaspora spreads into multitudes of forgotten areas in many service jobs. The Chinese underground church plans to send multitudes of Chinese believers to areas all along the Silk Road and "Back to Jerusalem".[iii] God is surely preparing the way for the fulfillment of the Great Commission and the return of His beloved Son.

The Church in every nation must consider its vital role in the Great Commission. Those nations who have seen themselves as receivers of message bearers, will have to embrace their call to be senders of message bearers. And each national church must focus on giving their student generation vision and identity in the overall mission movement. All too often this is neglected and can harm the mission movement as a whole.

Consider the small country of Armenia. Armenian believers would not typically have considered leaving their country as message bearers to other countries and/or ethnicities. I know one young Armenian, however, who was powerfully impacted at a YWAM Discipleship Training School in Europe. Upon her return to Armenia, she has shared the vision of global mission in University groups, and now many others are considering how they can become involved.

In Indonesia, a unified national student mission movement was launched in 2002. This movement influences many Indonesian college students to consider God's call upon their lives for the forgotten in their own country and beyond. Very few long-term Indonesian message bearers have ever been sent out. This movement is seeking to see 5,000 students raised up as long-term message bearers among the forgotten by 2010. Malaysia, a Muslim dominated country, also has a movement to see 10,000 Malaysian young adults (both Malay and Chinese) serving among the forgotten peoples of South East Asia by 2010.

God wants every non-western national church to mobilize and send their emerging generation through their own indigenous sending structures. Can you imagine it? Every national church sending cross-cultural message bearers into forgotten areas? Could we see the nations reached in our lifetime?

Take Brazilian outreach to Arabs in the Middle East, for example. Brazilians have the advantage of fitting in more easily there than white westerners do (their skin tone is similar to that of Arabs), and many are being received with open arms as Arabs feel a cultural connection with Latin Americans. Other Latin American nations are catching on to this strategy and also sending message bearers to the Middle East.

When a national church begins to focus on the forgotten outside of its borders, even though there is much to be done within them, God is glorified and will bring an outpouring within the borders as well. This is happening in many of the post-communist nations in Eastern Europe. Church leaders are catching a vision for how believers from their nations can be involved in global harvest. One ministry in Romania takes Romanian pastors to Northern India to expose them for the first time to the spiritual needs outside of their own country. They return with a vision to see message bearers sent out from their own congregations. Some of these new message bearers have been sent to work among Muslims in Turkey. The churches that send message bearers are revitalized as they pray for and give to these workers.

THE SCATTER PRINCIPLE

History shows that when God is ready to do something drastic, He tends to use the scatter principle. God loves to scatter His people from all kinds of backgrounds and mix them up in new surroundings in order to see the expansion of His Kingdom. You cannot be scattered, however, by choosing to remain at home. Oftentimes in history this has been done through persecution (Acts 8:4).

Winkie Pratney says about this scatter principle, "The gospel has always made greatest impact by an alien to a nation. A Jew brought it to Rome; a Roman took it to France; a Frenchman to Scandinavia; a Scandinavian to Scotland. A Scotsman took it to Ireland. The Englishmen, John Wesley and Whitfield took revival fire to America."[iv]

Strangers tend to gain a listening ear more readily than locals. The authority of a local is often ignored, as Jesus was rejected in his hometown. The mystery of a stranger claiming to have an important message can attract people.

HOW CAN GOD USE ME IN THE NATIONS?

The basic questions that the emerging generation across the globe is asking are "How can I be involved in cross-cultural ministry? What does it look like? What is really needed?" God has perfectly gifted His body so that every person will be interdependently involved in the Great Commission. The problem is that for too long we've not known how to use the gifts and abilities He bestows. Worse yet, we've often misused the gifts He has given us, stealing from the body the role He intended that we play in the Great Commission.

Church Planting

God's chief vehicle for reaching the world and manifesting His glory is church planting. We know that the local church is the mediator of God's work on earth, it is how He shows His glory to the world. To plant a church is to see the gospel take root in a place. Whereas evangelism brings light to individual people, church planting establishes the Kingdom of God in a place and brings corporate spiritual authority. Planting churches is an exciting and strategic way to see the kingdom come to the most forgotten areas of the world.

Each of us, however, holds a preconceived cultural idea of what a church is to look like and how it should function. Is a church a building, or can it gather under a tree, on a sidewalk, or in a slum? Is it at least fifty people coming together or do three brave Muslim background believers meeting in a basement constitute a church? Can it meet in a home? Does it need to have a contemporary worship leader with a guitar? Does a church in Iran or Libya look the same as one in Australia, England or Vietnam? Can a church be comprised of only children? These are questions that each church planting team must answer as they consider to which people God has called them, and the cultural context of that people.

Having a Platform

In most least-reached areas a church planting team will not be allowed to simply start evangelism meetings to find their foundation of a few believers with which to start a church. They must have a platform through which they can obtain a visa from the government, permitting them to live and work in the country. This platform can be anything, as long as the government sees it as legitimate and bringing benefit to the country. We must seek wisdom and creativity from God in this endeavor (James 1:5).

Many message bearers desire to use their college degrees to be involved in global proclamation. This is only logical as most of them have spent four years studying for their degree, and God can use their education in a very special way in the least-reached areas of the world. There are many examples of message bearers who work secular jobs, while also involved in a church planting effort or leading a Bible study for colleagues. It's time to overlook the traditional means of doing cross-cultural ministry and to allow the Holy Spirit to open our eyes to His new ways of taking this message to the forgotten.

Ministries to Consider

The following is a non-exhaustive list of possible ministries for message bearers. Each person must seek the Lord for creative and strategic ways of serving Him in the least-reached countries. In God's mind there are no closed countries. To enter and to remain without being kicked out, we need to be shrewd and wise, as Jesus exhorts us in Matthew 10:16, *"I am sending you out like sheep among wolves. Therefore be as shrewd as snakes and as innocent as doves."*

WORK WITH REFUGEES – There are millions of refugees around the world who have been displaced from their home country due to wars, famines, or natural disasters. Because many times they are in crisis, refugees are often open to gospel truth. Why not plant churches in a refugee camp in a forgotten area of the world?

WORK WITH AT-RISK CHILDREN – Street children, teenage prostitutes, prisons and orphanages all need to receive the love of Jesus. These young people often have no family, no income, and no hope. A network of ministries focusing on this large portion of humanity is the Viva Network. A good organization sending people to work among the poorest street children is Word Made Flesh.

OTHER JUSTICE ISSUES – There is injustice all over the world. Lawyers can use their skills to defend those who are being oppressed around the world. A particular group serving in this way is the International Justice Mission (IJM).

MEDICAL MISSIONS – This is a necessary and effective way to reach people for Christ. People in pain are very vulnerable and often open to hearing about what gives us hope. Long-term nurses and doctors are needed.

TEACHING ESL – People in almost every non-English speaking country want to learn English, as it is the universal business language and a ticket to better jobs. Teachers can develop deep friendships with, and communicate the love of Jesus to their students. All socio-economic levels of a society are open to English teachers.

TENTMAKING - USING COLLEGE DEGREES – This simply means using a degree to get a paying job in a foreign country with a national or international company, while working with a church planting team. Tentmakers can work as computer engineers, accountants, computer programmers, marketing directors, media specialists, business administrators , business consultants, economists, and much more.

TEACHING BIBLE TO NATIONAL BELIEVERS – Some who have degrees in Theology can join and/or start Bible schools for national pastors in countries where there is little training taking place. In the Arab world to have any kind of Bible college degree gives immediate respect among common people. One with a degree is immediately the "religious expert" even if he is a Christian. This provides many opportunities to answer questions and share the gospel.

HEALTH WORKERS – This includes teaching hygiene, principles of sanitation, and other ways of preventing illness. This kind of help is readily received in poverty-stricken areas, and is also welcomed by the government, often allowing a team to continue its church planting, even when an oppressive government is aware of it.

MICRO-ENTERPRISING–People do not usually have the initial capital needed to start a business, though it is usually only a couple hundred dollars, so message bearers can help small business owners get off their feet by providing a small amount of capital. This kindness paves the way for the message.

WATER PURIFICATION – Clean water is vital for good health, but many do not have clean water because they don't have basic wells or technology to clean their water. Message bearers can build wells and otherwise generate clean water.

SOCIAL WORKERS – There are troubled youth addicted to drugs and/or alcohol everywhere in the world. Why not go to them and work in their midst, eventually bringing them to the understanding of true hope in Jesus alone?

START A BUSINESS – Using whatever special skills one possesses and starting a business (a farm or orchard, a barbershop, a hair salon, a coffee house, a quilting business, a tourism business, etc) that can eventually employ nationals. This is a wonderful way to build relationships and get to know people. The barber shop in most places is the "gossip" center of town. Any skilled barbers?

LITERATURE AND BIBLE DISTRIBUTION – God has powerfully used His written word and other written materials to draw people to Himself. This kind of work tends to be "hit-and-miss", but effective when it hits. A good literature distribution ministry is Every Home For Christ. The Word of God is intrinsically powerful, and must get into the hands of people around the world. It truly is the best evangelist.

TEACHING IN UNIVERSITIES – Often, in certain countries, a message bearer can get a job as a professor with just a Bachelor's degree or a Master's degree. Message bearers are teaching economics, physics, chemistry and many other subjects in public universities as a way to build relationships and share the gospel.

COUNTRY ADVOCACY – There are places around the world where serious hardships are taking place that the outside world knows nothing about it. This type of work raises global awareness about certain areas and issues, ultimately benefiting the people living in that area.

BIBLE TRANSLATION – There are still multitudes of dialects and languages around the world that have no written Bible in their heart language. This will be the chief way that they will have the gospel proclaimed to them. It is urgent that we get the Bible translated. This is a very lengthy process and needs people who will commit to it for the long haul. Wycliffe Bible Translators is the primary translation organization.

GO AS A STUDENT – While an undergraduate or graduate student, this is a strategic way to connect with others in a given country. They often wonder why a westerner would come to study in their country, and it opens up ways to share Christ with them. Message bearer students can start mall churches in dorms.

TEACH LITERACY – Illiteracy is a major problem in many areas of the world, specifically among the forgotten. This provides much help to people and a potential listening ear for the message the message bearer came to bring.

USING THE CREATIVE ARTS – Though most of us in the Church haven't yet caught on, the creative arts are a powerful way in which to communicate the gospel. So many cultures in the world are oral learning cultures. They learn by telling stories and this opens up many doors for creative arts gifts. There is a vast array of creativity that has yet to be used to communicate the gospel throughout the earth.

PRIORITIZING THE FORGOTTEN

As we look at what remains in the task of global proclamation, it is absolutely critical that we focus our attention on those people and places where the gospel has had the least activity. It is to those who have had the least opportunity to hear the message of Life. Oswald J. Smith, founding pastor of the People's Church in Toronto in 1939, the first church ever to give 1 million dollars to cross-cultural ministry, was often heard saying, "No one has the right to hear the gospel twice, while there remains someone who has not heard it once."ᵛ I like to call these who are out of reach of any access to the gospel today the forgotten, though there are many other terms that would apply and that mean the same thing. The forgotten reminds me that these are people who have value as ones for whom Jesus willingly paid the ultimate price of giving His own life to deliver them from their bondage and sin. Yet, most of us in the body of Christ do not keep them or the need for their salvation at the forefront of our hearts, our prayer lives, or our mission-sending strategies, and therefore they have been forgotten by us.

Critics of this approach would say that to be strategic means we should go to people and places where there is a good response to the gospel. These proponents would say that this was what Jesus referred to when he taught about the good ground in His parables. Paul the Apostle, however, seemed to starkly disagree with this opinion, in Romans 15:20, *"It has always been my ambition to preach the gospel where Christ was not known."* And again in 2 Corinthians 10:16, *"...so that we can preach the gospel in the regions beyond you. For we do not want to boast about work already done in another man's territory."*

Paul's Motivation

Paul's heart cry was to see the transforming message of Truth get to those who had never heard it before. Was he just doing this so that he could take the credit for gospel work among them? Clearly not! He was driven by a love and commitment to Jesus to take the gospel to those who were beyond the gospel's previous reach. Why? Because Christ died to set them free, just as Paul had been set free from opposing Jesus and His followers (Acts 9:1-6).

Some might say that the gospel message has gone all over the world, and that there are no areas like this that remain. This statement could not be farther from the truth! Multitudes around the world have never heard about Jesus' love for them and His work on the cross. They might have heard of Christianity, but their definition of this would be far different from the truths that can set them free and change their lives. Like an untaught child, they are completely ignorant of truth in Jesus.

The forgotten are those who are from specific people groups around the world where the gospel has not yet taken root. However, this does not refer to a specific geographical place in the world. Because of globalization and people moving around to varying places, the forgotten can be found in Riyadh, Saudi Arabia; Tehran, Iran; Kuala Lumpur, Malaysia; Dhaka, Bangladesh; Sarajevo, Bosnia; Algiers, Algeria; Ho Chi Minh City, Vietnam; or Toronto, Ontario; Paris, France or Los Angeles, California. These need church planters who will focus all their energies upon them wherever they are located.

A message bearer who works among the Uygher people of Northwestern China took a four-month break from his work, returned to his hometown of Toronto, and found a Uygher community of several hundred. He prolonged his stay in Toronto and helped to establish a Uygher church.

HOW CAN I CULTIVATE VISION FOR THE FORGOTTEN?

How do we cultivate a vision right now wherever we are, for reaching the forgotten that need the life-changing power of Jesus Christ? Let me suggest several creative ways:

✔ Get a prayer calendar that highlights various people groups and consistently pray with insight and authority for them (www.calebproject.org).

✔ Adopt a forgotten people group and commit yourself to pray, give to those working among them, and mobilize your peers to consider working among them. (www.adoptapeople.org)

✔ Find and read books and biographies about cross-cultural ministry among forgotten people. (See Appendix A: Recommended Reading List)

✔ Reach out in love to international students in your community. Many internationals spend their entire time at a western university without ever being invited to someone's home.

✔ Use the daily "world" portion of the newspaper as a prayer guide for people around the world who are in turmoil and facing hardship.

✔ Commit to learn the language of a particular forgotten people and put an ad in your local newspaper to see if a native speaker can tutor you.

✔ Go on-line to "Google" and learn about any topic related to forgotten people.

✔ Look at the tags on the clothes in your wardrobe and each day pray for the country where your shirt was made. By doing this you will pray for nations containing some of the largest segments of forgotten people.

It is urgent that we focus our energies, our finances, and our time upon these people. We must do all we can to ensure that Jesus' incredible love is communicated in word and deed to these ones He loves so dearly, knowing that the day is coming to a close and that the night (when no man can work) is almost upon us (John 9:4).

---

i   Samuel Kang, *Missions Incredible*, Article in Christianity Today – March, 2006

ii   Timothy Olonade, *Nigerian Church takes the Gospel*...Article in Lausanne World Pulse, June, 2006

iii There are several books detailing the vision, motivation, and convictions of the Chinese underground church. A great one is *Back to Jerusalem* by Paul Hattaway

iv   Winkie Pratney, *Youth Aflame* (Minneapolis, MN: Bethany House Publishers, 1983) p. 148

v   Lois Neely, *Fire in his bones: The Official biography of Oswald J. Smith* (Wheaton, IL: Tyndale House Publishers, 1982) p.4

"Hear the sound of the Lion of Judah,

see the fire and the fear in the enemy's camp.

There's a new generation arising.

A nameless, faceless, placeless tribe.

All they fear is the Fear of the Lord,

all they hear is the Lion of Judah."

"To you I give my life.

Not just the parts I want to.

To you I sacrifice these dreams that I hold onto.

Your thoughts are higher then mine.

Your words are deeper then mine.

Your love is stronger then mine.

This is no sacrifice, here's my life!

To you I give my future, as long as it may last.

To you I give my present, to you I give my past."

JASON UPTON

---

[1] Jason Upton is a powerful worship leader with a prophetic gifting. His CDs are not your typical worship set,
but marked with Spirit-Led and lingering worship that touches the heart of God. His lyrics speak of God's ways
and plans for today's generation.

CONCLUSION
WHAT'S YOUR LIFE PURPOSE?

While sitting in a teaching session of my church's school of ministry a number of years ago, one of the pastors spoke about having a personal life purpose. At one point in the presentation he stopped and asked rhetorically, "What is your life purpose?" We each had generic Christian answers, but no specifics. He challenged us to ask God for a specific focus in order to be effective in ministry. It seems that all those who walked faithfully with God over a lifetime and were used by Him had a specific purpose.

Bobby Clinton defines a life purpose as: "A burden-like calling, a task or driving force or achievement, which motivates a person to fulfill something or to see something done.'" For many people, college is the ideal time to get the seeds of the vision for what God will call them to be about in life! He doesn't give us the whole picture all at once, for two reasons: first, because then life wouldn't require any faith, which would be in direct opposition to what the Bible calls us to, and second, because what He showed us would probably scare us half to death.

The first step to becoming aware of a life purpose is to surrender oneself and one's desires in life to God and be willing to be formed into the man or woman He has called us to be. It is not blind consideration or guesswork that determines what one is going to do with one's life. It is allowing Him to be Lord, the One who is in control.

Many of us may surrender to God, but we don't start moving when He stirs us in a particular way. We remain in the first step – surrender, when He calls us to the next step – discerning His call and moving in a specific direction. Because we like to keep our options open, and so we struggle with dedication, we need to receive direction from God, and then stick to it. This in no way means He won't clarify and redirect us along the way, but if we're not moving, how can He even do that?

As an illustration, nobody can turn a parked car. In the same way, God can't direct a person who isn't moving in some direction (even if it's the wrong way). If we are truly submitted to God, He will get us into the right place at the right time once we start moving in the vein of the burden He has already given us. We all must make decisions regarding our life and ministry. The best way to do this is in light of our understanding of who God has made us to be and for what purpose He is shaping us[ii].

The same pastor who challenged us to think about a life purpose then assigned us the task of creating a "Life Purpose Statement" according to what we knew God was calling us to do at that point in our lives. He reminded us that our life purpose might change in certain ways in the coming years, but that what was in our hearts presently would most likely only grow stronger and clearer in the future, rather than becoming dimmer and dimmer. He also gave some parameters, encouraging us to create our statement with focus, while keeping away from specifics like ministry names, specific churches, etc.

The Bible and church history are full of men and women who possessed a clear purpose in life that continually grew and to which they remained faithful. This helped them remain on target and not be swept away into jobs, roles, or concerns that were not relevant to the call and purpose that God had placed upon them. Circumstances might change, places of ministry might shift, but the heart and the convictions will remain the same.

It's Your Turn!

I want to invite each of us to sit down and write our own "Life Purpose Statement." What has God called us to be about in life and ministry? The things He has instilled in us already will help guide us. What gets us excited about serving God? When serving in a ministry, what are the types of things we like doing best (e.g., leading worship, speaking, praying, listening to people, administrating, helping behind the scenes, hospitality, dreaming up creative ideas for the ministry)? To what kinds of leaders or ministries are we most drawn? The answers to these questions can help us to identify the types of ministries in which we might one day participate. This is the "like-attracts-like" principle. Does our heart break for the homeless, for at-risk children, for child prostitutes in Southeast Asia, for the rich who are living empty lives? Are we hungry for more of God in our church or on our campus? These are simply start-up questions to get us thinking. Now is the time to choose to move in a direction that we sense God has put on our heart and to continually ask Him to unveil the next steps and clarify to us how we are move forward.

As an example, my life purpose statement is as follows:

"I purpose to be a man after God's own heart; to be a friend of His and a friend to my family. To be a servant to the nations devoted to equipping and calling the body of Christ to abandoned devotion and global proclamation. I commit to be a man of faithfulness and obedience unto Jesus, to fulfill what He has purposed for me, and to live life well and finish well as a child of the Most High God."

A TIME FOR ACTION...

The most dangerous thing to do now that we have read this book and recognized the heart-throbbing call of God to build the student mission movement campus by campus and country by country is...nothing. My prayer is that we have allowed our hearts to be challenged and motivated and our spirits to be invigorated, that we have captured a passion and vision for the things that God is passionate for, and caught a glimpse of how we can implement these ideas in our campus communities across the world. I invite us to respond to God right now! We cannot let an hour go by without spending time with Him, talking with Him, pouring our hearts to Him and consecrating ourselves to action in this pivotal hour of the church's existence.

I have great confidence that…

MANY OF YOU ARE GETTING READY TO TURN A CORNER IN ALL-OUT CONSECRATION, SURRENDER AND DAILY ABANDONED DEVOTION UNTO JESUS. MANY WILL BE MOTIVATED BY THE SPIRIT OF GOD TO PRAY LIKE NEVER BEFORE FOR THE FORGOTTEN, EVEN TO LAUNCH DAY AND NIGHT PRAYER ROOMS DEVELOPED ON YOUR CAMPUSES AND IN CHURCHES, AND TO GET MULTITUDES OF OTHERS INVOLVED IN CONSISTENT, ONGOING PRAYER ON BEHALF OF THE FORGOTTEN.

MANY WILL COMMIT TO STARTING A GRASSROOTS STUDENT MISSION INITIATIVE ON YOUR CAMPUS OR IN YOUR CHURCH'S COLLEGE AND CAREER MINISTRY, AND WILL SEE IT EXPLODE IN IMPACT.

MULTITUDES OF YOU WILL SIGN THE MESSAGE BEARER CREED COMMITTING YOUR LIVES TO GOD'S GLOBAL PURPOSE WITH THE FIRST STEP OF GOING FOR AT LEAST TWO YEARS, JOINING HUNDREDS OF YOUR PEERS AND WORKING TOWARDS THE GOAL OF 100,000 NEW MESSAGE BEARERS GOING OUT TO MAKE DISCIPLES AMONG THE FORGOTTEN.

As we move out to see the forgotten brought unto Jesus, may we take as many others with us as we possibly can as we build today's student mission movement! In the back few pages of this book are resources that are helpful in rebuilding the student mission movement on a campus or in a church community.

May God go before us as we launch out in abandoned devotion to Him and seek to build the student mission movement in our communities. …

---

i   Clinton's Biblical Leadership Commentary, p.515
ii Ibid, p. 516

APPENDIX A
RECOMMENDED READING

BIOGRAPHIES:

Anderson, Courtney. *To the Golden Shore:The Life of Adoniram Judson.*
Boston, MA; Little, Brown & Co., 1956.

Bauman, Dan. *Imprisoned in Iran.* Seattle, WA;YWAM Publishing, 1997.

Crossman, Eileen. *Mountain Rain:The Biography of James O. Fraser.*
United Kingdom; Paternoster Publishing, 2000

Edwards, Johnathan. *The Life and Diary of David Brainerd.* Massachusetts;
Hendrickson Publishers, 2006.

Elliot, Elisabeth. *A Chance to Die:The Life and Legacy of Amy Carmichael.*
Grand Rapids, MI; Revell House, 2005.

Grubb, Norman. *Rees Howells:Intercessor.* FortWashington, PA; CLC, 1997.

McClung, Floyd. *Living on the Devil's Doorstep.* Seattle, WA;YWAM
Publishing, 1999.

Muller, George. *The Autobiography of George Muller.* New Kensington, PA;
Whitaker House, 1984.

Olson, Bruce. *Bruchko.* Orlando, FL; Charisma House, 1977.

Roe, Earl, ed. *Dream Big! The Henrietta Mears Story.* Ventura, CA; Regal
Books, 1991.

Taylor, Dr. & Mrs. Howard. *Hudson Taylor's Spiritual Secret*. Chicago; Moody Publishers, 1955.

SPIRITUAL WARFARE & THE POWER OF THE HOLY SPIRIT:

Boyd, Gregory. *God at War*. Downers Grove, IL; InterVarsity Press, 1997.

Bush, Luis and Pegues, Beverly. *The Move of the Holy Spirit in the 10/40 Window*. Seattle, WA; YWAM Publishing, 1999.

Cho, David Yonggi. *The Holy Spirit, My Senior Partner*. Orlando, FL; Creation House, 1989.

Jacobs, Cindy. *Possessing the Gates of the Enemy*. Grand Rapids, MI; Chosen Books, 1994.

Kraft, Charles H. & Debord, David. *The Rules of Engagement*. Colorado Springs, CO; Wagner Publications, 2000.

Tozer, A.W. *Keys to the Deeper Life*. Grand Rapids, MI; Zondervan Publishing House, 1984.

White, Thomas. *The Believers Guide to Spiritual Warfare*. Ann Arbor, MI; Vine Books, 1990.

Wimber, John. *Power Evangelism*. London; Trafalgar Square Publishing, 2000.

Wink, Walter. *The Powers That Be*. New York; Galilee Books, 1998.

PRAYER:

Bounds, E.M. *Power Through Prayer*. New Kensington, PA; Whitaker House, 1983.

Duewel, Wesley. *Mighty Prevailing Prayer*. Grand Rapids, MI; Zondervan Press, 1990.

Engle, Lou. *Digging the Wells of Revival*. Shippensburg, PA; Revival Press, 1998.

Foster, Richard. *Prayer*. San Francisco, CA; Harper Collins, 1992.

Hattaway, Paul. *Operation China*. Pasadena, CA; William Carey Library, 2003.

Hayford, Jack. *Prayer is Invading the Impossible*. Orlando, Fl; Bridge-Logos Publishers, 2002.

Johnstone, Patrick & Mandryk, Jason. *Operation World*. Georgia; SendThe Light, 2001.

Murray, Andrew. *With Christ in the School of Prayer*. New Kensington, PA; Whitaker House, 1981.

Nee, Watchman. *Let Us Pray*. Richmond, VA. Christian Fellowship Publications, 1977.

Robb, John D. & Hill, James A. *The Peacemaking Power of Prayer*. Nashville, TN; Broadman & Holman Publishers, 2000.

Sheets, Dutch. *Intercessory Prayer*. Ventura, CA; Regal Books, 1996.

SHARING JESUS WITH...

...Muslims

Accad, Fuad. *Building Bridges*. Colorado Springs, CO; NavPress, 1997.

Adeney, Miriam. *Daughters of Islam*. Downers Grove, IL; InterVarsity Press, 2002.

Braswell Jr., George W. *Islam: Its Prophet, Peoples, Politics, and Power*. Nashville, TN; Broadman & Holman Publishers, 1996.

Brother Andrew. *Light Force*. Grand Rapids, MI; Revell Books, 2004

Gabriel, Mark A. *Islam & the Jews*. Orlando, FL; Charisma House, 2003.

Greenlee, David, ed. *From the Straight Path to the Narrow Way*. Waynesboro, GA; Authentic Media, 2005.

Livingstone, Greg. *Planting Churches in Muslim Cities*. Grand Rapids, MI; Baker House, 1993.

Mallouhi, Christine. *Waging Peace on Islam*. Downers Grove, IL; IVP, 2002.

Muller, Roland. *Tools for Muslim Evangelism*. Ontario, Canada; Essence Publishing, 2000.

Musk, Bill. *Touching the Soul of Islam*. Grand Rapids, MI; Monarch Books, 2005.

Zwemer, Samuel. *Islam and the Cross*. New Jersey; P & R Publishing, 2002.

...Buddhists:

Hale, Thomas. *A Light Shines in Central Asia: A Journey into the Tibetan Buddhism World*. Pasadena, CA; William Carey Library.

Lim, David & Spaulding, Steve. *Sharing Jesus in the Buddhist World (vol. 1, 2, 3)*. Pasadena, CA; William Carey Library, 2003.

...Hindus:

Bharati, Dayanand. *Living Water and Indian Bowl*. Pasadena, CA; William Carey Library, 2004.

Hoeffer, Herbert. *Churchless Christianity*. Pasadena, CA; William Carey Library, 2002.

REVIVAL CLASSICS:

Burns, James. *Revivals: Their Laws and Leaders*. Grand Rapids, MI; Baker Book House, 1960.

Cairns, Earle E. *An Endless Line of Splendor*. Illinois; Tyndale House, 1986.

Gillies, John. *Historical Accounts of Revival*. New York; Banner of Truth, 1981.

Lloyd-Jones, Martin. *Revival*. Wheaton, IL; Crossway Books, 1987.

Lyall, Leslie T. *John Sung: Flame for God in the Far East*. Chicago; Moody Press, 1964.

Ravenhill, Leonard. *Why Revival Tarries*. Minnesota; Bethany House Publishers, 2004.

Ryle, J. C. *Christian Leaders of the 18th Century*. Pennsylvania; Banner of Truth, 1978.

Shear, John. *Old Time Revivals*. New York; Million Testaments Campaign, 1932.

Wallis, Arthur. *In the Day of Thy Power*. Fort Washington, PA; CLC, 1990.

APPENDIX 6
QUOTES TO INSPIRE & ACTIVATE US

"It is possible for the most obscure person in a church,
with a heart right toward God,
to exercise as much power for the evangelization of the world,
as it is for those who stand in the most prominent positions."
JOHN R. MOTT

"God has huge plans for the world today!
He is not content to merely establish a handful of struggling churches
among each tongue, tribe and nation.
Even now He is preparing and empowering His Church
to carry the seeds of revival to the uttermost ends of the earth."
DAVID SMITHERS

"I have but one candle of life to burn,
and I would rather burn it out in a land filled with darkness
than in a land flooded with light"
JOHN KEITH FALCONER

"The Bible is not the basis of missions;
missions is the basis of the Bible"
RALPH WINTER

*"Missionary zeal does not grow out of intellectual beliefs,
nor out of theological arguments, but out of love."*
ROLAND ALLEN

*If missions languish, it is because the whole life of godliness is feeble.
The command to go everywhere and preach to everybody is un-obeyed,
until the will is lost by self-surrender in the will of God.
There is little right giving because there is little right living,
and because of the lack of sympathetic contact with God in holiness of heart,
there is a lack of effectual contact with him at the Throne of Grace.
Living, praying, giving and going will always be found together,
and a low standard in one means a general debility
in the whole spiritual being."*
ARTHUR T. PIERSON

*"I used to think that prayer should have the first place
and teaching the second.
I now feel it would be truer to give prayer
the first, second and third places and teaching the fourth."*
JAMES O. FRASER

*"Forbid that we should ever consider
the holding of a commission from the King of Kings a sacrifice,
so long as other men esteem the service of an earthly government as an honor.
I am a missionary, heart and soul.
God Himself had an only Son, and He was a missionary and a physician.
A poor, poor imitation I am, or wish to be, but in this service I hope to live.
In it I wish to die.
I still prefer poverty and mission service to riches and ease.
This is my choice!"*
DAVID LIVINGSTONE

*"He is no fool who gives what he cannot keep
to gain what he cannot lose."*
JIM ELLIOT

*"In every revival there is a reemphasis of the Church's missionary character.
Men return to Calvary, and the world is seen afresh through the eyes of Christ.
The infinite compassion of Christ fills the heart,
and the passion evoked by Calvary demands the whole wide world
as the fruit of His sacrifice."*

JOHN SHEARER

*"It is utterly impossible to divorce the story of student awakenings
from the course of missions in countries overseas.
From the beginning, one of the most immediate and
dramatic effects of college revivals
has been the recruitment of personnel
for the work of Christ abroad."*

J. EDWIN ORR

*"The main reason we should be praying about revival
is that we are anxious to see God's name vindicated and His glory manifested.
We should be anxious to see something happening that will arrest the nations,
all the peoples, and cause them to stop and think again."*

MARTIN LLOYD-JONES

*"The chief danger of the Church today
is that it is trying to get on the same side as the world,
instead of turning the world upside down.
Our Master expects us to accomplish results,
even if they bring opposition and conflict.
Anything is better than compromise, apathy, and paralysis.
God give to us an intense cry
for the old-time power of the Gospel and the Holy Ghost!"*

A. B. SIMPSON

*"Have you noticed how much praying for revival has been going on of late -
and how little revival has resulted?
I believe the problem is that we have been trying to substitute praying for obeying,
and it simply will not work.
To pray for revival while ignoring the plain precept laid down in Scripture
is to waste a lot of words and get nothing for our trouble.
Prayer will become effective when we stop using it as a substitute for obedience."*

A. W. TOZER

APPENDIX C

WHAT IS SVM2?

Student Volunteer Movement 2 (SVM2) is an informal network of students, leaders, churches, and organizations serving a grassroots mission movement among today's emerging generation toward the fulfillment of the great commission in our lifetime.

This is accomplished in unity by:

1) Challenging the emerging generation to abandoned devotion to Jesus Christ and sacrificial living for the sake of the gospel.

2) Cultivating a prayer movement for the nations – campus by campus.

3) Facilitating campus mission initiatives resulting in multitudes of laborers being sent to the least-reached via their local churches or partnering agencies.

4) Equipping students and leaders with practical resources and training for the student mission movement.

5) Networking like-minded students, leaders, churches and organizations around a common mission vision.

How Can I Get Involved As A Student?

SVM2 is a grassroots movement across the student world implemented within existing ministry structures on Christian college campuses, within campus ministry organizations, and in local churches. You, as a student, are the centerpiece of this initiative. Things happen as you take the vision, strategies, and materials and integrate them into your local church and college campus! A place to start is by considering your own convictions regarding God's call to reach the world. Consider signing the **Message Bearer Creed**. Next, open your heart to get God's vision for influencing your community with spiritual revival that leads to multitudes committing to their role in the Great Commission. Start one or more Global Prayer Teams in your community and get a hold of the Movement Manual to see step by step how to move your campus community toward a thriving student mission initiative.

How Can I Get Involved As A Mission Agency Mobilizer?

As an advocate of the movement, you participate by challenging students with a common vision of a united movement among the emerging generation in order to reach the world for Christ in our lifetime. This is done through encouraging students in your databases to implement the various resources. The identity of belonging to something bigger then themselves and creating a sense of mission momentum across organizations is our aim. Will you help build this movement? SVM2 is not a sending structure of any sort, but instead challenges students to make spirit-led, faith-filled commitments to give themselves fully to Jesus and to serve among the forgotten. Challenge students you meet to sign the Creed and connect with a movement of their peers, and then talk to them about the opportunities to serve in your organization. This commitment materializes as they connect with a mission sending agency or structure that fits their circumstances, vision, and gifts.

What Can I Do As A Campus Ministry Staff Person?

Most of the resources have been developed with you in mind. We know how busy it can be to lead a campus ministry fellowship. These resources help you to implement solid student mission vision into your community and watch it take off. You are encouraged to get some student leaders together and challenge them to launch out with these materials and vision and develop a student mission initiative within your campus ministry fellowship. In doing so, your students connect with a widespread informal movement that is arising toward these ends.

What Can I Do As A Local Church Leader?

The local church is the key to students being sent out in droves to the nations. Too often, students go off to college and leave behind their local church altogether. This causes many local churches to have a tough time keeping a college group together. We want to encourage the development of this movement in local churches. Get a hold of the materials and use them to stimulate the hearts of your young adults. Connect with students and start Global Prayer Teams, hold meetings focused on learning about the state of global proclamation today, and so much more. God wants to infuse local church college ministries with His fire and passion for the nations, using them to stimulate greater mission vision in the church as a whole.

What Can I Do As A Mission Mobilization Ministry?

You are already being used of God to stir hearts with His global passions! You are encouraged to use the Message Bearer Creed in your presentations and call students to spirit-led, faith-filled decisions and to stick with them unless the Lord leads otherwise. This is a natural way to create a common mission challenge among the emerging generation. Many are using the Creed with powerful results. Get a hold of these cards on the website. Affiliate yourself with the SVM2 network through putting the logo on your website and talking about its vision and values (it is a vision and values driven movement) during your presentations. Encourage the formation of Global Prayer Teams and campus mission initiatives and the connecting and networking of these through the SVM2 website.

MATERIALS & RESOURCES

All of these resources can be ordered at www.SVM2.net.

ABANDONED TIMES
E-BULLETIN

The **Abandoned Times** is an email bulletin with encouraging and inspiring articles related to the building of today's student mission movement. Articles focus on developing abandoned devotion to Jesus and accomplishing the global proclamation of the gospel in our lifetime.

Sign up for a free subscription at
www.svm2.citymaker.com/page/page/2004142.htm.

Tell your friends about it as well....

ARE YOU
A MESSAGE BEARER?

Message Bearer Creed:

By God's grace as a Message Bearer, I covenant to:

Abandoned Devotion:

Wholeheartedly devote myself to the person of Jesus Christ and be committed to the marks of a true disciple.

Global Proclamation:

Sacrificially pursue revival and the spread of the gospel in the midst of the forgotten, through disciplined prayer, giving, and the commitment to go for two years or more.

Spread the Vision:

Intentionally influence others to develop an awareness of the global purpose of God toward the aim of personal involvement.

Join with hundreds of students and young adults around the world stating their intention to do their part in reaching the nations for Christ by becoming a Message Bearer. To make this commitment go to www.SVM2.net, click on the link to Message Bearers, and follow the simple instructions.

Use the Message Bearer Creed to challenge your friends with long-term commitment to serve among forgotten peoples of the world. The Message Bearer Creed exists for a three-fold purpose:

1. To bring a common cross-cultural ministry challenge to the student world.

2. To connect isolated young adults who make the commitment with a network of others around the world doing the same thing.

3. To increase the number of students making long-term commitments and build momentum toward a pervasive movement.

GLOBAL PRAYER TEAMS GUIDE

The **Global Prayer Team Guide** envisions and equips students to start, invigorate and maintain a small group committed to ongoing, sacrificial intercession for our generation to reach the nations. It details steps for holding effective corporate prayer meetings fixated on the nations regularly while encouraging their use in a widespread manner across campuses and in local churches, creating momentum.

THERE IS A DEVOTED PRAYER MOVEMENT FOR THE NATIONS RISING....WILL YOU HELP CHANGE NATIONS?

MOVEMENT MANUAL

The **Movement Manual** equips student leaders, who possess a passion for influencing their peers with global mission vision, with ideas, examples, and steps to follow in developing a thriving student mission movement in their community. These are timeless principles to implement that impact and catapult a community forward with spiritual vibrancy and contagious vision to reach the nations.

THE MOVEMENT MANUAL IS A WEALTH OF IMPARTATION FOR THOSE READY TO GO TO THE NEXT LEVEL.

ABANDONED DEVOTION GATHERING FACILITATION PACK

The **Abandoned Devotion** Gathering Facilitation Pack provides all of the materials (DVD Clips, powerpoints with prayer topics, schedules, explanation of every portion of the gathering and how to facilitate it, etc.) necessary for a five-hour corporate prayer and worship event focused on the nations hosted on campuses and in churches. Abandoned Devotion Gatherings are for the purpose of deliberately seeking God through extended worship, uncompromising challenges, and radical prayer to see the message of Jesus spread globally in our lifetime.

GET THE PACK AND IMPLEMENT THESE GATHERINGS REGULARLY ON YOUR CAMPUS AND WATCH HOW LIVES ARE CHANGED.

IGNITE TRAINING WEEKENDS

IGNITE Training Weekends bring together, envision, and equip student leaders from various campuses, organizations, and churches who possess a passion to practically move toward a renewed student mission movement today within each of their respective ministries. The main curriculum of the weekend is the Movement Manual.

As students take a passion for Jesus and subsequent mission vision to a deeper level on their campus, the student mission movement is rebuilt. This happens as they challenge their ministries and campuses practically with God's purpose of global proclamation and implement key strategies for fruitfulness.

The purpose of IGNITE is to equip student leaders with spiritual formation, leadership development, practical, effective ideas and strategies to increase mission vision on campus, and give them the opportunity to connect with other student leaders and form relationships. IGNITE is a challenge to take the idea of a widespread student mission movement out to other campuses and churches.

WANT TO HOST A WEEKEND?
CONTACT US AT INFO@SVM2.NET

THE GO MOBILIZATION PACKET

The **GO Packet** is a tool for short-term mission trip leaders to use on the field to challenge their students to long-term involvement among the forgotten. Knowing that most short-term mission experiences are intense and leaders are often very busy with trip details, the GO Packet allows a vision for long-term ministry to be integrated 'right out of the box,' during a short-term trip utilizing audio CDs and debrief questions, with only minimal preparation.

The core messages (each one hour in duration) are:

1. **THE REASON:** The Biblical Basis of Mission — Calling, skill-sets and missions - Is a specific personal calling to involvement in God's global purpose needed?

2. **THE NEED:** The Unreached — Interactive activity focusing on the questions: what is the 10-40 window, are there still people who have never heard of Christ and the gospel and do we still need longer-term workers from the West?

3. **THE CALL:** A Short Term Trip is Not Enough — What would going for longer-term look like? What type of people does God use? What type of people is the world crying out for? Could I be a Message Bearer to the forgotten?

The GO Packet is a great tool to help your short-term mission program have a longer- term impact by casting a vision of the broader picture of God's global purpose and helping to catalyze long-term mission commitment.

HAYSTACK PACK
(DVD & STUDY GUIDE)

This DVD and Study Guide give you all that you need to tell the story of the 1806 Haystack Prayer Meeting and apply its lessons for today. The Haystack DVD details the story and gives the historical background of how God used five young underclassman to birth the foreign mission movement in North America. The video can be used effectively in both a large group and small group setting.

The accompanying study guide walks you through six key lessons from the Haystack Prayer Meeting that can be learned and applied today – designed to help your church or fellowship catch a vision for the role that prayer plays in global mission and launching movements that impact God's kingdom. This six-lesson study guide helps to lay a foundation for starting and sustaining a global prayer team that meets regularly to intercede for our generation to reach the nations.

The Haystack DVD and Study Guide is an excellent first step toward establishing a prayer group for the nations as well as a great study to incorporate in an existing prayer group to reinvigorate and envision those praying with some of the great stories of how God has used the intersection of prayer, students and obedience to birth movements that have changed the world.

APPENDIX E

WEB RESOURCES

24-7 Prayer - *www.24-7prayer.com*

International House of Prayer — Kansas City - *www.fotb.com*

The Traveling Team — *www.thetravelingteam.org*

Mission Network News - *www.mnnonline.org*

Perspectives - *www.perspectives.org*

Campus Transformation Network — *www.campustransformation.com*

Crescent Project — *www.crescentproject.org*

Joshua Project — *www.joshuaproject.net*

Caleb Project — *www.calebproject.org*

The Journey Deepens — *www.thejourneydeepens.com*

Urbana — *www.urbana.org*

Wake and Go — *www.wakeandgo.org*

BIBLIOGRAPHY

Bonhoeffer, Dietrich. *The Cost of Discipleship.* New York: The McMillan Co., 1963.

Brown, Michael. *Revolution! The Call to Holy War.* Ventura, CA: Regal Books, 2000.

Bush, Luis & Beverly Pegues. *The Move of the Holy Spirit in the 10/40Window.* Seattle, WA: YWAM Publishing, 1999.

Clinton, Richard & Paul Leavenworth. *Starting Well.* Altadena, CA; Barnabas Publishers, 1994.

Clinton, Robert J. *Clinton's Biblical Leadership Commentary.* Pasadena, CA: Fuller Publishing, 2002.

_____ *Clinton's Nehemiah Leadership Commentary.* Pasadena, CA: Barnabas Publishers, 2002.

Cunningham, Loren. *Making Jesus Lord.* Seattle, WA: YWAM Publishing, 1988.

Eastman, Dick. *Change the World School of Prayer Manual.* Every Home For Christ International, 1991.

Engle, Lou. *"Dreams."* Harvest Rock Church, March 10, 2002. Preaching Audio Tape.

Gabriel, Mark, *Islam and the Jews.* Lake Mary, FL: Charisma House, 2003.

Greenway, Roger, John Kyle, & Donald McGavran. *Missions Now: This Generation*. Grand Rapids, MI: Baker Book House, 1990.

Greig, Pete. *Awakening Cry*. London, England: Silver Fish Publishing, 1998.

Howard, David. *Student Power in World Evangelism*. Downers Grove, IL: Inter-Varsity Press, 1970.

Joyner, Rick. *The Surpassing Greatness of His Power*. Charlotte, NC: Morning Star Publications, 1996.

Markert, Fred. *Global Strategic Mission*. CDTS sessions at Kona YWAM Base, 2004. Teaching CD.

McClung, Floyd. "Apostolic Passion." Article in *Perspectives on the World Christian Movement: A Reader*. Pasadena, CA: William Carey Publishers, 1999.

McQuilken, Robert. *The Great Omission*. Grand Rapids, MI: Baker House, 1984.

Mears, Henrietta, C. *What The Bible Is All About*. Wheaton, Ill: Tyndale Publishers, 1987.

Morgan, G. Campbell. *Handbook for Bible Teachers and Preachers*. Grand Rapids, MI: Baker Book House, 1994.

Murray, Andrew. *The Key to the Missionary Problem*. Fort Washington, PA: CLC Publications, 1979.

Neely, Lois. *Fire In His Bones: The Official Biography of Oswald J. Smith*. Wheaton, IL: Tyndale House, 1982.

Norton, Wilbert. *To Stir the Church*. Madison, WI: Self-Published by Student Foreign Missionary Fellowship (SFMF), 1986.

Olson, Bruce. *Bruchko*. Lake Mary, FL: Charisma House, 1977.

Pierson, Paul. MH520 Lecture Notes – "Historical Development of the Christian Movement." Pasadena, CA: Fuller Theological Seminary – Individualized Distance Learning.

Piper, John. *Let The Nations Be Glad*. Grand Rapids, MI: Baker Books, 1993.

Pratney, Winkie. *Fire on the Horizon*. Ventura, CA: Renew Books, 1999.

_____*Youth Aflame*. Minneapolis, MN: Bethany House Publishers, 1983.

Shadrach, Steve. *The Fuel and the Flame*. Waynesboro, GA: Authentic Lifestyle, 2003.

Shibley, David. *The Missions Addiction*. Lake Mary, Fl: Charisma House, 2001.

Sider, Ronald. *Rich Christians in an Age of Hunger*. Dallas, TX: Word Publishing, 1997.

Smithers, David. *"Revelation and Revival."* Teen Mania Missions Conference, 2001. Preaching Audio Tape.

Taylor, Dr. & Mrs. Howard. *Spiritual Secret of Hudson Taylor*. New Kensington, PA: Whitaker House, 1996.

Tozer, A. W. *The Divine Conquest*. Camp Hill, PA; Christian Publications, 1950.

_____ *Of God And Men*. Harrisburg, PA: Christian Publications Inc., 1960.

Verwer, George. "Address at the World Consultation on Frontier Missions, Edinburgh, 1980." Article in *Seeds of Promise*. Allan Starling, ed. Pasadena, CA: William Carey Publishers, 1981.

Van Engen, Charles. MT542 *Course Reader*. Pasadena, CA: Fuller Theological Seminary, 2001.

Wallstrom, Timothy. *The Creation of a Student Movement to Evangelize the World*. Pasadena, CA: William Carey Publishing, 1980.

Witherall, Gary. *Total Abandon*. Wheaton, IL: Tyndale House, 2005.